PRACTICAL 30 DAY

PALEO PROGRAM

FOR WEIGHT LOSS

'A BEGINNER'S GUIDE TO HEALTHY RECIPES FOR WEIGHT LOSS

AND OPTIMAL HEALTH'

Elizabeth Vine

FOR ALL YOUR DIETARY PLANNING NEEDS.

CONTENTS

WELCOME TO THE PRACTICAL 30 DAY PALEO PROGRAM!

FIRST OF, CONGRATULATIONS, ON MAKING THE CHOICE TO EAT CLEANER & HEALTHIER!

THIS GUIDE IS DESIGNED TO PROVIDE WITH YOU ALL THE TOOLS, RECIPES AND PLANS YOU NEED TO EAT REAL FOODS FOR 30 DAYS STRAIGHT. THE CHALLENGE IS SPECIFICALLY TAILORED TO GET YOU TO SHOP, COOK, EAT AND THINK PALEO FOR 30 DAYS. THE WEIGHT LOSS, HEALTHIER SKIN, BETTER SLEEPS, HIGHER LEVELS OF ENERGY AND VARIOUS OTHER BENEFITS WILL FOLLOW ON ITS OWN.

WE'VE BROKEN IT DOWN TO A VERY EASY TO FOLLOW SCHEDULE INCLUDING A SHOPPING LIST OF ESSENTIALS TO GET YOU STARTED. THE ITEMS LISTED ON THE GETTING STARTED SHOPPING GUIDE WILL LAST YOU THE FULL 30 DAYS, REPLENISHMENTS FOR A FEW ITEMS THAT WILL RUN OUT ARE INCLUDED IN YOUR WEEKLY SHOPPING GUIDE.

THE WEEKLY SHOPPING GUIDE OUTLINES EVERYTHING YOU'LL NEED TO GET ON YOUR SUNDAY NIGHT GROCERY SHOP FOR THE WHOLE WEEK AS PER THE RECIPES ON THE CALENDAR.

THE RECIPES FOR THE WEEK ARE WRITTEN, IN ORDER OF THE CALENDAR, FOLLOWING THE

WEEKLY SHOPPING GUIDE. JUST FLIP THE PAGE AND FOLLOW THE RECIPE WHEN YOU'RE READY FOR YOUR NEXT MEAL!

**ALL THE RECIPES ARE FOR 2-3 SERVING SIZES. IF YOU'RE DOING THIS ON YOUR OWN, JUST CUT EVERYTHING IN HALF OR FREEZE EXTRAS. REMEMBER, ANY DINNER LEFTOVERS CAN BE EATEN FOR BREAKFAST/LUNCH THE NEXT DAY, EXTENDING THE 30 DAYS.

WE'VE TAKEN ALL THE THINKING OUT OF COOKING FOR THE NEXT 30 DAYS FOR YOU SO SAVE THIS TO YOUR KINDLE, TABLET, IPAD, PHONE, OR PRINT AND STICK IT ON THE FRIDGE, AND FOLLOW ALONG.

YOU'LL START TO FEEL RESULTS BY WEEK 2 AND SEE HOW DELICIOUS AND EASY IT IS TO EAT PALEO!

LOVES,

**PALEO WIRED
GATHER.EAT.REPEAT.**

www.paleowired.com

GETTING STARTED SHOPPING GUIDE

You may already have a number of the items on this list at home saving you time and money when you do your first grocery shop! We recommend you print this and tick off everything on this list, then purchase the remaining items.

And remember, if it's not on this shopping list or the weekly shopping lists following, it's best to set the remaining items aside deep in the pantry – or if you're 100% committed donate or toss them, along with a few other steps which we outline at GOING PALEO.

GETTING STARTED SHOPPING GUIDE:

1 PACKAGE OF ORGANIC BLACK PEPPER
1 PACKAGE OF MEDITERREANIAN SEA SALT
1 SMALL PACKAGE OF ORGANIC DRIED CHILI FLAKES
1 PACKAGE OF ORGANIC PARSLEY FLAKES
1 PACKAGE OF ORGANIC DRIED OREGANO
1 SMALL PACKAGE ORGANIC GARLIC POWDER
1 SMALL PACKAGE OF ORGANIC CAYENNE PEPPER
1 SMALL PACKAGE ORGANIC THYME
1 SMALL PACKAGE ORGANIC PAPRIKA
1 SMALL PACKAGE ORGANIC CUMIN
1 SMALL PACKAGE PUMPKIN SPICE
1 SMALL PACKAGE ORGANIC CINNAMON
1 SMALL PACKAGE ORGANIC NUTMEG
1 SMALL PACKAGE ORGANIC SAGE

1 PACKAGE BAKING POWDER
1 PACKAGE BAKING SODA

1 SMALL JAR NO MSG MUSTARD
8OZ (250ML) APPLE CIDER VINEGAR
1 BOTTLE COLD PRESSED ALL NATURAL OLIVE OIL
1 BOTTLE OF FRYING OIL OF CHOICE (coconut or avocado recommended)
1 SMALL 8OZ (250G) JAR OF COCONUT OIL
1 BOTTLE ALL NATURAL NO MSG FISH SAUCE
1 SMALL JAR GREEN CURRY PAST (preservative & sugar-free, recommended THAI KITCHEN)
1 SMALL PACKAGE COCONUT AMINOS

1 8OZ (250G) JAR OF RAW HONEY
1 8OZ (250ML) BOTTLE ALL NATURAL ORGANIC MAPLE SYRUP

1 SMALL BOTTLE ALL NATURAL VANILLA EXTRACT
1 SMALL PACKAGE SHREDDED COCONUT FLAKES
1 SMALL PACKAGE OF ARROWROOT POWDER
1 LB PACKAGE ALMOND FLOUR/MEAL
1 LB PACKAGE COCONUT FLOUR

1 SMALL PACKAGE CHIA SEEDS
1 SMALL PACKAGE HEMP SEEDS

1 STICK OF GRASS-FED BUTTER
1 8OZ (250G) JAR OF ALMOND BUTTER

1 2L UNSWEETENED ALMOND MILK

WEEK #1
MEAL CALENDAR

	BREAKFAST	LUNCH	DINNER
MONDAY	Scrambled Eggs & Bacon	Turkey Patties	Chicken Alfredo & Bacon
TUESDAY	Eggs & Sweet Potato Hashbrowns	Chicken Salad with Bacon, Avocado and Tomatoes	Paleo Pizza
WEDNESDAY	Get up & Go 2 minute Smoothie	"Leftover" Paleo Pizza	Wild Sockeye Salmon
THURSDAY	Paleo Granola & Fruit	Bacon Asparagus Wrap w/ Roasted Vegetables	Shrimp Salad
FRIDAY	Pumpkin Muffins	Tomato Soup & Tuna Salad	Beef & Broc Stir-fry
SATURDAY	Mushroom Egg Frittata	Zucchini Pad Thai	Good Ole Meatloaf
SUNDAY	Coconut Blueberry Pancakes	Shrimp, scallops & crab with Veggie Patties	Cauli Rice & Green Curry

WEEK#1
SHOPPING LIST

*FRUITS & VEGETABLES ALL ORGANIC AND/OR WILD
*MEATS FREE RANGE, NO ANTIBIOTICS OR HORMONES ADDED
*FISH OCEAN WISE & WILD
*Remember to always read the ingredients and check for added sugars, chemicals and MSG etc.

1 LEMON
2 LIMES
4 MEDIUM YELLOW ONIONS
1 BUNDLE ORGANIC GREEN ONIONS
1 RED ONION
1 GINGER ROOT
2 WHOLE GARLIC
1 BUNDLE OF ASPARGUS
2 CAULIFLOWER HEADS
2 ORGANIC RED PEPPERS
2 GREEN PEPPERS
3 AVOCADOS
1 PACK BOK CHOY
15 ORGANIC TOMATOES
1 SPAGHETTI SQUASH
3 SWEET POTATOES
1 YAM
2 BUNDLES OF ORGANIC BROCCOLI
6 ZUCCHINI
4 CARROTS
3 BEETS
12-15 BROWN MUSHROOMS
1 SMALL BAG/BOX ARUGULA SALAD
1 BUNDLE OF ROMAINE LETTUCE
1 BUNDLE FRESH BASIL

2 APPLES
1 BANANA
1 SMALL PACKAGE FRESH OR FROZEN WILD BLUEBERRIES
1 ORANGE

2 PACKAGES FREE RANGE NO ANTIOBIOTIC EGGS (24 TOTAL)

1 20oz (750Ml) TOMATO SAUCE
1 CAN 14OZ TOMATO PUREE
2 8oz (250mL) CANS COCONUT CREAM
2 16oz (500mL) CANS COCONUT MILK
1 12OZ CAN PUMPKIN PUREE

JAR OF OLIVES (no sugars added)

1 - ½ LB SMALL BAG (200G) OF REAL CRAB MEAT
2 – 2 LB BAGS (400G EACH) OF FROZEN WILD SHRIMP & SCALLOP MEDLEY
1 LARGE PIECE WILD SOCKEY SALMON (FRESH)
1 LB BEEF SIRLOIN
1LB GROUND BEEF
1 ½ LB (750G) NO-ANTIOBIOTIC CHICKEN SLICES
4 NO-ANTIOBIOTIC ALL NATURAL CHICKEN BREAST
7OZ (400G) ORGANIC GROUND TURKEY
1 PACKAGE MSG-FREE, NO NITRATE BACON

100G DRIED FRUIT (BLUEBERRIES, CRANBERRIES)
200G HAZELNUTS
100G ALMONDS
100G CASHEWS
100 WALNUTS
100G SESAME SEEDS
50G PUMPKIN SEEDS

1 BOTTLE NO SULFITE ORGANIC WHITE WINE (OPTIONAL)

WEEK #1
RECIPES

Breakfast: Scrambled Eggs & Bacon

SERVES: 1-2
PREP TIME: 5 min
COOK TIME: 5 min

Ingredients:
2 eggs
two slices of bacon
1/2 avocado
1 tomato
Salt
Pepper

Directions:
1. Place 2 slices of bacon into a frying pan at medium heat.
2. Flip after 1 minute on each side, repeating until cooked to desired crunch-factor!
3. Remove bacon from the pan and put on a plate, leaving the grease behind.
4. Crack each of the 2 eggs directly into the pan.
5. Cook the eggs for about 3 minutes; once done take out of the pan and place on a plate.
6. Wash and cut tomato into bite size pieces and add to plate.
7. Dice the avocado and add to plate. Add salt & pepper to taste.
8. Serve & Enjoy!

Lunch: Turkey Patties

SERVES: 3-4
PREP TIME: 25 min
COOK TIME: 15 min

Ingredients:
400g (7oz) ground turkey
1 medium onion
2 garlic cloves
400g (14 oz) tomato puree
1 egg
1 tsp hemp seeds (optional)
2 Tbsp Avocado Oil
1tsp dried parsley
1tsp Chilli flakes
Salt
Pepper
2 oz of water
Directions:
1. Chop the onion into small pieces.
2. Mince the garlic.
3. Combine the ground turkey meat with onion, garlic, egg, hemp seeds, and teaspoon of chilli flakes, salt and pepper into one bowl.
4. Mix well.
5. Leave in the fridge for 20 minutes.
6. Remove from fridge and make into patties.
7. Heat the oil over medium heat in a frying pan.
8. Once oil is hot, place the Patties and cook 4 minutes/side.
9. Turn to low temperature and add the tomato puree (optional) over the patties in the pan.
10. Cook another 3 minutes.
11. Serve & Enjoy!

Dinner: Chicken Alfredo + Bacon

SERVES: 2
PREP TIME: 5 min
COOK TIME: 25 min

Ingredients:
½ LB (250g) chicken slices
1 cup heavy coconut cream
2 Tbsp butter
4 tsp Arrowroot Powder
1 tsp garlic powder
Salt
Pepper
2 slices of bacon
1 spaghetti squash
2 Tbsp Avocado Oil
Directions:
1.   In a medium saucepan, add the coconut cream, butter, arrowroot powder, garlic powder and 1 tsp salt and pepper.
2.   Heat over medium temperature carefully stirring the ENTIRE time with a whisk until everything thickens. Put aside and keep warm.
3.   In a frying pan, add 2 slices of bacon on medium heat and cook until crispy for 4-5 minutes.
4.   Remove the bacon from the pan and leave the grease. Cut the slices of bacon into small 1" pieces.
5.   Add the chicken slices and cook covered for 4-5 minutes in the bacon grease.
6.   Flip the chicken and cook for another 3-4 minutes until cooked all the way through.
7.   Cut the spaghetti squash lengthwise and remove all seeds from the middle.
8.   Put ½ inch of water into a microwaveable plate, and place 1 half of the cut squash face down.
9.   Microwave for 6-8 minutes.
10.   Leave to sit for a few minutes then use a fork to separate out the spaghetti strands.
11.   Repeat with the remaining spaghetti squash.
12.   Add the spaghetti squash, bacon pieces and chicken to the Alfredo mixture.
13.   Mix well.
14.   Serve & Enjoy!

Breakfast: Eggs & Sweet Potato Hash browns

SERVES: 2-3
PREP TIME: 5-10 min
COOK TIME: 40 min

Ingredients:
2 sweet potatoes
1 medium onion
3 eggs
2 Tbsp Avocado Oil
Salt
Pepper
1 tsp chilli flakes
1 green onion
Directions:
1. Preheat oven to 400F.
2. Wash the sweet potatoes and cut off the ends.
3. Using a sharp knife and leaving the skin on, cut up the sweet potatoes into small squares.
4. In a bowl add 3 Tbsp of oil to the chopped sweet potato squares, and add 1 tsp of salt, pepper and chilli flakes.
5. Spread onto a baking sheet, evenly distributing, and cook in the oven for 20-25 minutes. Mix and flip at the 15min mark.
6. When sweet potatoes are done, put into a frying pan or skillet and make three small spaces in the pan.
7.Over low-med heat, directly crack 3 eggs into the space and cook on the stove for 10-15min until eggs are set.
8. Wash and finely chop 1 green onion.
9. Top with green onion bits and a sprinkle of salt and pepper.
10.Serve & Enjoy!

Lunch: Chicken Salad with Bacon, Avocado and Tomatoes

SERVES: 2-3
PREP TIME: 5 min
COOK TIME: 30 min

Ingredients:
4 small pieces of chicken breast
1 bundle of Romaine Lettuce
2 tomatoes
4 slices of bacon
2 Tbsp Avocado Oil
Pepper
Salt
Cold pressed olive oil, drizzled

Directions:
1. Cut the chicken breast into small pieces and add a bit of salt and pepper.
2. Heat the oil in a pan over medium temperature.
3. Add the chicken breasts into the pan and fry until golden brown (25-30 min), flipping often.
4. Wash and cut the lettuce into bite sized pieces and place into a bowl.
5. Wash and slice the tomato and add to the salad bowl.
6. Dice avocado and add to salad bowl.
7. Place 4 slices of bacon into microwave for 4-5 minutes.
8. Chop the bacon slices into small pieces and add to the salad bowl.
9. Once chicken is cooked, add to the salad bowl.
10. Add salt, pepper and mix well. Drizzle with olive oil to taste.
11. Serve & Enjoy!

Dinner: Paleo Pizza

SERVES: 2-3
PREP TIME: 5 min
COOK TIME: 35-40 min

Ingredients:
1 large head of cauliflower
2 eggs
1 ½ cups tomato sauce
Zucchini
2 Green peppers
1 red or orange pepper
8-10 green olives (optional)
Dried Oregano
Salt
Pepper
Directions:
1. In a large saucepan bring 3L of water to a boil over medium heat.
2. Wash the head of cauliflower and cut off all green stems.
3. Add the head of cauliflower to the boiling water and cook for 7-8 minutes.
4. Drain EXTREMELY well. The more drained and moisture removed from the cauliflower the better the quality of your pizza crust!
5. Cut into small florets and in a food processor or using a grater make the cauliflower into a rice-like texture.
6. In a bowl, add 2 eggs, salt and pepper and mix together well.
7. On a pizza pan, pour out your pizza 'crust'.
8. Heat oven to 400F, and bake pizza 'crust' for 20min in the oven until starts to turn slightly brown.
9. Wash and cut the peppers and zucchini.
10. Cover pizza 'crust' with tomato sauce, spread evenly, and add zucchini and peppers as toppings.
11. Add olives and top with dried oregano.
12. Put back in the oven and bake for another 10 minutes.
13. Serve & Enjoy!

Breakfast: Get up & Go 2 minute Smoothie

SERVES: 2
PREP TIME: 2 min
COOK TIME: *none

Ingredients:
1/2 cup frozen mixed berries
1/3 cup raw beet
1" piece of ginger root
1 tsp honey
1 apple
Handful of ice cubes
1/4 cup almond or coconut milk
2 tsp Chia seeds
Directions:
1. Combine all ingredients in a blender or magic bullet.
2. Blend and it's ready!
3. Serve & Enjoy!

Lunch: **last night's leftover Paleo Pizza!

Dinner: Wild Sockeye Salmon

SERVES: 2-3
PREP TIME: 5 min
COOK TIME: 25 min

Ingredients:
1 large fresh piece of Wild Sockeye Salmon
2 Tbsp Avocado Oil
Salt
Pepper
1 Tbsp Mustard
2 lemon wedges
3 cups arugula salad, washed
Directions:
1. Heat the oven to 400F.
2. Grease a baking sheet with oil.
3. Place salmon on baking sheet and rub with oil.
4. With a teaspoon, cover top of salmon facing up with mustard.
5. Add salt and pepper and juice of 2 lemon wedges.
6. Place in oven and cook uncovered for 20 - 25 minutes.
7. Check every 10 min.
8. When Salmon flakes easily with fork and the top is lightly brown, it's done.
9. Allow to sit for 2 minutes, then cut into 3-4 pieces and serve on a bed of arugula salad.
10. Serve & Enjoy!

Breakfast: Paleo Granola & Fruit

SERVES: 2-3
PREP TIME: 5 min
COOK TIME: *none

Ingredients:
1/4 cup almonds
1/4 cup cashews
1/2 cup hazelnuts
1/3 cup dried fruit (blueberries, cranberries etc)
1 Tbsp pumpkin seeds
1 Tbsp coconut flakes
1 Tbsp honey
1 orange
1 tsp Chia
1 apple or peach
1 banana
Almond milk
Directions:
1.   In a blender or magic bullet, combine almonds, cashews and hazelnuts.
2.   Mix for 30 seconds until small pieces but before it starts to butter.
3.   Put into a bowl and add the dried fruit, pumpkin seeds, coconut flakes.
4.   Squeeze juice of 1 orange and add to the bowl.
5.   Add honey, chia and slice apple (or peach) and banana and add to the bowl.
6.   Fill bowl with almond milk like you would with a bowl of cereal.
7.   Serve & Enjoy!

Lunch: Bacon Asparagus Wrap w/ Roasted Vegetables

SERVES: 2-3
PREP TIME: 5-7 min
COOK TIME: 45 min

Ingredients:
1 yam
1 sweet potato
2 beets
medium onion
1 bunch of asparagus
5 slices of bacon
Salt
Pepper
2 tsp Chilli flakes
2 tsp Dried oregano
2 Tbsp Avocado Oil
Directions:
1. Preheat oven to 425F.
2. Wash yam, sweet potato, and beets.
3. Using a sharp knife, chop the yam, sweet potato and beets into bite-sized chunks. Try to keep them all consistent size so they cook evenly!
4. Cut the onion into square sized chunks.
5. Add 3 tablespoons of oil and salt, pepper and chilli flakes.
6. Mix well together in a large bowl coating all the vegetables.
7. Put into a baking dish, spreading evenly and cover with aluminum foil.
8. Cook for 25-30 minutes, and check by piercing with a fork. The fork should easily pierce any of the vegetables.
9. Remove foil, and cook for another 5 minutes.
10. Wash the asparagus stalks, and cut the 1/4" of the stalk bottom off piercing little Xs on each bottom with a knife.
11. Cut each bacon slices into 3 equal sized pieces.
12. Use each of the now 15 bacon pieces to wrap around a stalk of asparagus diagonally.
13. When vegetables are done, remove and set aside, lowering the oven temperature to 400F.
14. Put the bacon wrapped asparagus on a baking dish placing side by side, careful not to overlap any of the pieces.
15. Cook in the oven for 5 minutes, then remove and flip.
16. Cook for another 5-7 minutes until bacon is cooked and asparagus is easily pierced with a fork.

17. Serve & Enjoy!

Dinner: Shrimp Salad

SERVES: 2-3
PREP TIME: 5-7 min
COOK TIME: 15 min

Ingredients:
1-1 LB package of frozen wild shrimp
1 avocado
1 cup arugula salad
2 tomatoes
2 Tbsp Avocado Oil
Pepper
Salt
Cold Pressed olive oil
Directions:

1. Heat the oil in a frying pan over low to medium temperature.
2. Remove shrimp from package and in a bowl, run cold water over top for   3-5 minutes.
3. Add the shrimp to the frying pan and cook for 10-15 minutes at medium temperature, stirring frequently.
4. In a salad bowl, add arugula salad pieces.
5. Cut up the tomatoes and add to the salad bowl.
6. Dice the avocado and add to the salad bowl.
7. Add salt, pepper and cold pressed olive oil to taste.
8. Add the shrimp.
9. Mix altogether well.
10. Serve & Enjoy!

Breakfast: Pumpkin Muffins

SERVES: 2-3
PREP TIME: 5 min
COOK TIME: 15-20 min

Ingredients:
1/2 cup coconut flour
1 12oz can pumpkin puree
6 eggs
1/4 cup honey
1/4 cup walnuts
3 tsp pumpkin spice
1 tsp baking powder
½ cup Coconut oil
2 tsp vanilla extract
Directions:
1. Preheat oven to 400F.
2. In a medium sized bowl add coconut flour, pumpkin spice, 1/4 cup walnuts and baking powder together.
3. In another bowl, add 3/4 cup pumpkin puree, 1/2 cup of melted coconut oil, 6 eggs, 2 tsp vanilla extract, 1/4 cup honey and mix well.
4. Add the dry ingredients to the mixture and combine well.
5. Grease a muffin tray with coconut oil.
6. Pour batter into the muffin tray tins and bake 15-17 minutes or until thoroughly cooked.
7. Serve & Enjoy!

Lunch: Tomato Soup & Shrimp Salad

SERVES: 2-3
PREP TIME: 10 min
COOK TIME: 20 min

Ingredients:
**leftover shrimp salad from last night
2 Tbsp coconut oil
5 garlic cloves
3 lbs tomatoes
Fresh basil
1 cup all natural chicken broth
2/3 cup coconut milk
Salt
Directions:
1. Mince the garlic cloves.
2. In a medium saucepan over low heat, add the garlic cloves.
3. Cook for no more than 1 minute.
4. Wash and cut the tomatoes into large pieces.
5. Add the tomatoes to the pan.
6. Add 5 fresh basil leaves.
7. Add chicken broth and coconut milk and mix well.
8. Cook over medium heat for 20 minutes or so.
9. Remove from heat and let cool for 5-10 minutes.
10. Using a magic bullet, immersion or regular blender mix everything until smooth and no more chunks remain.
11. Pair with leftovers from last night's shrimp salad!
12. Serve & Enjoy!

Dinner: Beef & Broc Stir-fry

SERVES: 4
PREP TIME: 3 min
COOK TIME: 20 min

Ingredients:
3 Tbsp Avocado Oil
1 LB beef sirloin
Head of broccoli
Red bell pepper
2 carrots

1 green onion
2 garlic cloves
2 Tbsp sesame seeds
2 Tbsp Coconut aminos (paleo soy sauce!)
Directions:
1. Cut the 1lb beef sirloin into strips around 2" thick.
2. Wash and cut the broccoli, red pepper, carrots and green onion.
3. Mince the garlic.
4. In a medium saucepan, heat 3 tablespoons of oil on medium-high temperature.
5. Add the beef strips and cook for 3-4 minutes, until seared brown.
6. Remove the beef and put on a plate on the side.
7. In the same oil, add all the cut vegetables and cook for 2-3 minutes.
8. Stir beef into the vegetables and add 2 Tbsp coconut aminos and 2 Tbsp sesame seeds.
9. Cook until all vegetables are tender and meat is fully cooked.
10. Serve & Enjoy!

Breakfast: Mushroom Egg Frittata

SERVES: 2-3
PREP TIME: 3 min
COOK TIME: 12-15 min

Ingredients:
12-15 brown mushrooms
2 tomatoes
1 red onion
1 garlic clove
8 eggs
Salt
Pepper
Parsley
2 Tbsp Avocado Oil
Directions:
1. Heat 1 Tbsp of oil over medium temperature in an oven-safe saucepan.
2. Using a wet paper towel wipe clean the mushrooms and cut into slices.
3. Wash and cut the tomatoes into circular slices.
4. Chop 1/2 cup of red onions.
5. Into the saucepan add the mushrooms, tomato slices and red onion and cook 3-4 minutes.
6. In a separate bowl whisk eggs with 1 Tbsp water, and 1 tsp salt, pepper and parsley.
7. Stir the cooked vegetables into the bowl.
8. Heat another 1 Tbsp of oil over medium temperature.
9. Add the entire mixture and cook 5-6 minutes until the bottom starts to turn brown.
10. Put into oven under broil from 3-4 minutes.
11. Serve & Enjoy!

Lunch: Zucchini Pad Thai

SERVES: 2-3
PREP TIME: 5 min
COOK TIME: 20 min

Ingredients:
1/4 cup coconut or avocado oil
3 zucchinis
1 medium onion
1 garlic clove
1 tablespoon apple cider vinegar
1 ginger root
1 Tbsp Almond butter
1 Tbsp Chilli paste
1 Tbsp Fish sauce
1 lime, juiced
Salt
Pepper
Directions:
1.   Slice the zucchinis very thinly length-wise with a sharp knife or mandolin and put into a bowl.
2.   Chop the onion and mince the garlic.
3.   Peel and cut up 1"x1" of the ginger root, mincing into small pieces.
4.   In a medium frying pan, heat 2 Tbsp of oil over medium temperature.
5.   Add the onion, garlic and ginger and cook 3-5 minutes until soft.
6.   Add 1 tablespoon of fish sauce, chilli paste, apple cider vinegar, juice of 1 lime, almond butter and a pinch of salt.
7.   Mix everything together well in the pan and cook for 5 minutes.
8.   Add the zucchini noodles to the pan and stir in well, cooking for another 10 minutes.
9.   Serve & Enjoy!

Dinner: Good Ole Meatloaf

SERVES: 2-3
PREP TIME: 10 min
COOK TIME: 50 min

Ingredients:
1lb ground beef
2 cups almond flour
1 can coconut milk
2 garlic cloves
2 carrots
1 medium onion
1 zucchini
1 egg
Parsley flakes
Oregano flakes
Chilli flakes
Salt
Pepper
2 Tbsp Avocado Oil
Directions:
1. Preheat Oven to 350F.
2. In a medium bowl, add 1/3 cup coconut milk and 2 cups almond flour and mix well.
3. In a large saucepan, heat 3 tablespoons of oil over medium heat.
4. Dice ½ an onion.
5. Wash and chop zucchini and carrots.
6. Mince the garlic.
7. In the saucepan, add carrots, onion, zucchini and garlic for 5-7 minutes.
8. Remove sautéed vegetables from heat and put aside.
9. Add the vegetables into the bowl of coconut milk and almond flour.
10. Add the ground beef, egg, 1 tsp each of parsley, oregano, chilli flakes, salt and pepper and mix well.
11. Grease a loaf pan and pour mixture into it, spreading evenly.
12. Cook for 45-50 minutes in the oven.
13. Serve & Enjoy!

Breakfast: Coconut Blueberry Pancakes

SERVES: 2-3
PREP TIME: 5 min
COOK TIME: 10 min

Ingredients:
4 eggs
1 cup almond milk
2 Tbsp honey
1 tsp vanilla extract
1/2 cup coconut flour
1 tsp baking soda
Salt
1 cup blueberries
3 Tbsp Avocado Oil
Directions:
1. In a medium sized bowl, whisk the eggs, milk, honey and vanilla together.
2. In a separate bowl, add the coconut flour, baking soda, and salt together.
3. Add the wet mixture to all the dry ingredients and stir in the blueberries.
4. In a medium saucepan, heat 3 Tbsp of oil over medium heat.
5. Pour batter into pan over hot oil, usually 2 will fit side by side.
6. Once bubbles start to appear on the top of the pancake, 2 minutes or so, flip to other side until golden brown.
7. Repeat with the remaining batter until all the pancakes are cooked.
8. Option to top with banana slices, almond butter or maple syrup!
9. Serve & Enjoy!

Lunch: Shrimp, scallops & crab with avocado, tomato, vegetable Pattie & asparagus

SERVES: 2-3
PREP TIME: 10 min
COOK TIME: 40 min

Ingredients:
1 – 1LB bag of frozen wild shrimps and scallops
1 – ½ LB bag of frozen real crab meat
1 garlic clove
1 avocado
1 tomato
2 Tbsp Avocado Oil
2 tsp Pepper
1 tsp Salt
4 asparagus stalks
2 tsp Italian parsley
2 oz White wine (optional)
For the Veggie Patties:
2 carrots
2 celery sticks
1 zucchini
1 egg
1 tbsp of coconut flour
1 chilli pepper
1 pepper (green or red)
1 1" piece fresh ginger root
1 garlic clove
black pepper
salt
2 Tbsp Avocado Oil
Directions:
1. Mince the garlic clove.
2. Remove the shrimp, scallops and crab from package and run under cold water for 3-5 minutes in a big bowl.
3. Over medium temperature, put a tablespoon of oil to heat.
4. Add garlic and sauté the garlic until it's soft, not brown.
5. Add shrimp, scallops and crab meat.
6. Add salt, Pepper and Italian parsley.
7. Add 1 oz of water into the pan.
8. Add 2 oz of white wine (optional, if you're going clean you can use clam juice).

9. Cook for 20 minutes.

10. To make the patties, grate the vegetables ingredients above and put into one large bowl.

11. Add the egg, and salt and pepper to taste.

12. Mix well together.

13. Using your hands roll out small-medium sized patties.

14. On low temperature, heat the oil in a frying pan.

15. Place patties (4 at a time should fit) in the pan and cook each side for 4-6 min.

16. Flip patties to other side and cook for another 4-6 min.

Once first round of patties is done, repeat the process for the rest.

17. Wash asparagus, and cut the ends making an X on the bottom of each stalk with a sharp knife.

18. Place on a baking sheet and lightly pour oil, sprinkling with salt and pepper.

19. Place into the oven at 350F for 5-10 min.

20. When the seafood is done serve with avocado, tomato, roasted asparagus and veggie patties.

21. Serve & Enjoy!

Dinner: Cauli Rice & Green Curry

SERVES: 4
PREP TIME: 5 min
COOK TIME: 30 min

Ingredients:
Head of cauliflower
1/3 cup water
Cayenne pepper
Parsley
Salt
Pepper
Green curry paste (preservative & sugar-free)
1 LB chicken slices
2 cups coconut cream
1 Tbsp fish sauce
1 lime
Broccoli head
1 zucchini
1 pack bok choy
3 Tbsp Coconut oil
Directions:
1. Grate the florets of the cauliflower into small pieces.
2. Add the grated cauliflower into a pan filled with 1/2 cup water and cook on medium temperature for about 10 minutes.
3. Add a tsp each of cayenne pepper, parsley, salt and pepper to the cauliflower once it's soft.
4. In a large saucepan, over medium heat add 3 Tbsp coconut oil.
5. Add 3 Tbsp green curry paste and cook for 2-3 minutes.
6. Add the sliced chicken slices and cook until golden brown 5-7 minutes, stirring often.
7. Wash and cut vegetables into bite-sized pieces.
8. Add the coconut cream, fish sauce and vegetables.
9. Cook for 7-10 minutes until vegetables are fully cooked.
10. Leave on the side for 5 minutes letting all the flavours combine.
11. Dish out cauliflower rice and top with chicken green curry.
12. Serve & Enjoy!

WEEK #2
MEAL CALENDAR

	BREAKFAST	LUNCH	DINNER
MONDAY	Mushroom Bacon & Eggs	Curry Chicken Salad	Meat & Potato Bake
TUESDAY	Green Smoothie	Sweet Potato Salad with Roast Chicken	Paleo Jambalaya
WEDNESDAY	Breakfast Wrap	Kale Salad with Avocado Dressing	Acorn Squash & Pork Chops
THURSDAY	Summer Fruit & Nut Butter Smoothie	Chicken Salad with Bacon, Avocado & Tomatoes	Baked Sweet Potato
FRIDAY	Banana Bread w/ Coconut Butter	Beef & Broc Stir-fry	Swiss Chard & Sweet Potato Goodness
SATURDAY	Veggie Patties	Chicken Burgers & Guacamole	Mexican style Salad
SUNDAY	Avocado Sunny Side UP! Eggs	Mussels	Casserole Cave-style sans the Cheese

Week#2
SHOPPING LIST

*FRUITS & VEGETABLES ALL ORGANIC AND/OR WILD
*MEATS FREE RANGE, NO ANTIBIOTICS OR HORMONES ADDED
*FISH OCEAN WISE & WILD
*Remember to always read the ingredients and check for added sugars, chemicals and MSG etc.

1 ORGANIC LEMON
2 LIMES
1 ACORN SQUASH
1 BUNCH ORGANIC KALE
1 ORGANIC ROMAINE LETTUCE
1 ORGANIC SWISS CHARD
1 BUNDLE FRESH SPINACH LEAVES
1 BUNDLE ORGANIC BROCCOLI
2 CAULIFLOWER HEADS
5 ORGANIC CELERY STICKS
1 ORGANIC CHILI PEPPER
5 MEDIUM ONIONS
1 BUNDLE GREEN ONIONS
1 RED ONION
2 WHOLE GARLIC
2 RED BELL PEPPERS
8 GREEN BELL PEPPERS
1 YELLOW BELL PEPPER
1 ZUCCHINI
4 CARROT STICKS
8 MEDIUM ORGANIC SWEET POTATOES
8 ORGANIC AVOCADOES
5 ORGANIC TOMATOES
20-23 ORGANIC BROWN MUSHROOMS
1 SMALL BUNDLE FRESH CHIVES
1 SMALL PACKAGE CORIANDER LEAVES
1 PACKAGE FRESH DILL
1 BUNDLE ORGANIC FRESH CILANTRO
1 BUNDLE ORGANIC FRESH PARSLEY

2 ORGANIC RED APPLE
7 ORGANIC BANANAS
1 SMALL PACKAGE PITTED ORGANIC DATES

2 PACKAGES FREE RANGE NO ANTIOBIOTIC EGGS (24 TOTAL)

1 15OZ BOTTLE DICED TOMATOES
1 JAR NO SUGAR, PRESERVATIVE FREE SALSA (OR MAKE YOUR OWN FROM PALEOWIRED.COM)
1 PACKET NO MSG TACO SEASONING
1 SMALL CAN COCONUT CREAM

1 PACKAGE MSG-FREE, NO NITRATE BACON
8 OZ ORGANIC SPICY SAUSAGE (YOUR CHOICE)
5 NO-ANTIOBIOTIC ALL NATURAL CHICKEN BREASTS
1 LB GROUND ORGANIC CHICKEN
1 2LB NO-ANTIOBIOTIC ALL NATURAL WHOLE CHICKEN
2 SMALL ORGANIC PORK CUTLETS
1/2 LB LEAN ORGANIC GROUND PORK
2 1/2LB ALL NATURAL GROUND BEEF
2LB (1KG) ALL NATURAL ROAST BEEF
1LB ALL NATURAL BEEF SIRLOIN
1LB OCEAN WISE SHRIMP, PEELED AND DEVEINED
4 1/2 LB (2KG) OF WILD MUSSELS

100G PECANS
100G RAISINS
100G WALNUTS
1 SMALL PACKAGE GROUND FLAXSEEDS

1 BOTTLE NO SULFITE ORGANIC WHITE WINE (OPTIONAL)

WEEK #2

RECIPES

Breakfast: Mushroom & Bacon Eggs

SERVES: 2-3
PREP TIME: 5 min
COOK TIME: 10 min

Ingredients:
2 eggs
500g of fresh mushrooms
2 slices of bacon
1 avocado
Salt
Pepper
1 tsp Mustard
2 Tbsp Avocado Oil
Directions:
1. Clean and slice mushrooms.
2. Over medium temperature, heat oil in the pan.
3. Add mushrooms and cook for 6 min. Take out of the pan and add eggs, cooking for 5-6 min, until eggs are done to your liking.
4. Add salt and pepper to taste.
5. Place 2 slices of bacon into microwave for 2-3 minutes.
6. Dice the avocado.
7. Serve eggs with mushrooms on a plate with bacon slices and avocado. Top with mustard.
8. Serve & Enjoy!

Lunch: Curry Chicken Salad

SERVES: 2-3
PREP TIME: 5 min
COOK TIME: 15 min

Ingredients:
1 chicken breast
1 celery stick
1 red apple
1/2 cup pecans
1/2 cup raisins
1/4 cup coconut cream
2 Tbsp curry paste
Salt
Pepper
1 tsp Cayenne pepper
2 Tbsp Avocado Oil

Directions:
1. In a medium saucepan, heat 2 Tbsp of oil over medium temperature.
2. Grill the chicken breast, 5-6 minutes on each side ensuring it's cooked all the way through.
3. Slice the chicken breast into bite sized pieces and put aside.
4. Wash and dice the celery stick into very small pieces.
5. Wash and cut 1/2 a red apple into very small pieces.
6. Chop the pecans with a knife into small pieces.
7. In a medium bowl add the chicken breast pieces, diced celery, red apple pieces and pecans.
8. Add the raisins, 1 tsp of cayenne pepper, salt and pepper.
9. In a small bowl, combine 1/4 cup coconut cream with 2 Tbsp curry paste.
10. Mix the two together well and add to bowl with all other ingredients.
11. Stir well together coating with curry sauce.
12. Serve & Enjoy!

Dinner: Meat & Potato Bake

SERVES: 2-3
PREP TIME: 10 min
COOK TIME: 60-75 min

Ingredients:
2 LB roast beef
2 sweet potatoes
1 medium onion
2 garlic cloves
1 Tbsp cold pressed olive oil
Salt
Pepper
Directions:
1. Preheat oven to 350F.
2. Place the roast beef (best if it's at room temperature) into a large baking dish.
3. Cut the onion into quarters and add to the dish.
4. Wash the sweet potatoes and cut into 1"x1" cubes. Add to the baking dish.
5. Add the garlic cloves whole to the baking dish.
6. Stir the potatoes, onions and cloves around the roast beef with 1 Tbsp olive oil.
7. Sprinkle with salt and pepper.
8. Cook for 60-75 minutes.
9. Serve & Enjoy!

Breakfast: Green Smoothie

SERVES: 2
PREP TIME: 5 min
COOK TIME: *none

Ingredients:
2 bananas
1 cup ice
2 leaves kale
1 avocado
1 date
1/3 cup water

Directions:
1. Combine all ingredients in a blender or magic bullet.
2. Blend and optional: top with chia or hemp seeds.
3. Serve & Enjoy!

Lunch: Sweet Potato Salad w/ Roast Chicken

SERVES: 2-3
PREP TIME: 10 min
COOK TIME: 60 min

Ingredients:
1 2lb whole chicken
1 onion
2 sweet potatoes
4 hard boiled eggs
2 celery sticks
1/4 cup fresh dill
1/3 cup cold pressed olive oil
1/4 cup red onion
2 cloves garlic
Pepper
Salt

Directions:
1. Preheat the oven to 400F.
2. Rinse the whole chicken and dry well with a paper towel.
3. Rub salt and pepper over the whole chicken.
4. Using twine, bring the wings and legs close to the body of the chicken and tie the ends of the drumsticks together. This helps to cook more evenly.
5. Put into a roasting pan, and with the legs facing you put the chicken into the pan.
6. Cover and cook in the oven for 1 hour.
7. Remove and baste with 1 Tbsp of unpasteurized butter.
8. Preheat the oven to 350F (you can also cook the sweet potato at the same time as the chicken for 40-45 minutes)
9. Wash the sweet potatoes and puncture with a fork all around the thickest part.
10. Wrap in aluminum foil and bake for 50-60 minutes until fully cooked.
11. Cool the sweet potatoes and cut into cubes.
12. In a large salad bowl, add the cubed sweet potatoes and chopped hard boiled eggs.
13. Wash and chop the celery sticks and chop the red onion. Add to the bowl.
14. Chop the dill and add 1/4 cup to the bowl.

15. Add 1 tsp salt, pepper and minced garlic cloves.
16. Add the 1/3 cup olive oil and mix well altogether.
17. Serve & Enjoy!

Dinner: Paleo Jambalaya

SERVES: 4
PREP TIME: 10 min
COOK TIME: 45-50 min

Ingredients:
8 oz spicy sausage of choice
1 red pepper (orange or green OK)
1 yellow pepper
4 garlic cloves
1 onion
1 15oz can diced tomatoes
1 Tbsp paprika
1 tsp thyme
1 tsp cumin
1 tsp cayenne pepper
1 1/2 cups all natural chicken broth
1 cauliflower head
1 lb shrimp, peeled and deveined
Salt
Pepper
Fresh cilantro
Directions:
1. In a large saucepan, heat 2 Tbsp oil over medium heat.
2. Add sliced sausage and cook for 4-5 minutes until it starts to brown.
3. Wash and dice the peppers and add to the pan.
4. Mince the garlic cloves and add to the pan.
5. Add ½ the onion and stir everything together, cooking for another 3-4 minutes.
6. Stir in the diced tomatoes, paprika, thyme, cumin, cayenne pepper, salt and pepper.
7. Add the chicken stock and bring to a boil.
8. Once boiling, turn the heat down and simmer for 20 minutes.
9. Wash the cauliflower head and using a food processor or grater - grate into a rice like consistency.
10. Mix in 1/2 of the cauli rice and simmer for 12-15 minutes altogether.

11. Add the shrimp and cook another 5-7 minutes.
12. Add salt and pepper to taste.
13. Chop fresh cilantro and sprinkle on top.
14. Serve & Enjoy!

Breakfast: Breakfast Wrap

SERVES: 1
PREP TIME: 5 min
COOK TIME: 20 min

Ingredients:
1 egg
1 egg white (additional)
2 tsp ground flaxseed
Salt
1 avocado
3 eggs
1 red pepper
Spinach leaves
2 slices bacon
1/4 cup salsa
2 Tbsp Avocado Oil
Directions:
1. Preheat the oven on broil.
2. In a bowl, add 1 egg, 1 egg white, 2 tsp ground flaxseed and a pinch of salt.
3. Mix well.
4. Heat 2 Tbsp of oil over medium heat in a medium saucepan or non-stick skillet.
5. Pour half the mixture into the pan and distribute evenly cooking for 2-3 minutes until bottom is golden brown.
6. Using a spatula, loosen the tortilla from the pan without flipping.
7. Place the entire pan into the oven and leave for 3-4 minutes until the top becomes bubbly. Remove from pan, your wrap is ready to go!
8. In the same pan, place 2 slices of bacon and cook 3-4 minutes on each side until crispy. Set aside.
9. Wash and dice the red pepper and wash the spinach leaves.
10. Without remove grease from the pan, add the pepper and cook for 2 minutes.
11. Crack 3 eggs directly into the pan and add the spinach leaves.
12. Cook altogether for 3-4 minutes until eggs are scrambled and spinach is soft.
13. Slice ½ an avocado into long slices.
14. In the breakfast wrap, place the egg mixture, 2 slices of bacon, sliced avocado and 1/2 cup of paleo salsa.
15. Serve & Enjoy!

Lunch: Kale Salad with Avocado Dressing

SERVES: 2-3
PREP TIME: 10 min
COOK TIME: *none

Ingredients:
1 bunch of kale
1 apple
1/2 cup walnuts
1 Tbsp olive oil
1 lemon
1 avocado
1/4 cup water
1 lime
1 Tbsp maple syrup
1 tsp cumin
2 Tbsp coriander leaves
Salt
Pepper
Directions:
1. Wash the kale and remove the stalks.
2. Tear into bite sized chunks into a large bowl and add olive oil and juice of 1/2 a lemon and mix well.
3. Chop 1/2 cup of walnuts and add to mixture.
4. Wash and cut the apple into slices, adding to mixture.
5. In a blender or magic bullet, add 1 avocado, 1/4 cup water, juice of 1 lime, 1 Tbsp maple syrup 1 tsp cumin, 3 Tbsp coriander leaves and 1 tsp of salt and pepper.
6. Blend well until a completely smooth texture.
7. Pour the dressing over the salad and mix well.
8. Serve & Enjoy!

Dinner: Acorn Squash & Pork Chops

SERVES: 2
PREP TIME: 5 min
COOK TIME: 40 min

Ingredients:
2 pork cutlets
Olive oil
Salt
Pepper
1 acorn squash
2 Tbsp pasteurized butter
1 tsp Garlic powder
1 tsp Salt
1 tsp Pepper
½ tsp Thyme
Directions:
1. Rub salt and pepper onto pork cutlets.
2. Pour olive oil on both sides of cutlets and rub in well.
3. Light the BBQ and heat up to a medium flame.
4. Put the pork cutlets on the BBQ.
5. Cook 12 min on each side, checking every 5 min.
6. Add tsp of olive oil as needed during cooking.
7. Preheat oven to 400 degrees.
8. Cut acorn squash in half, lengthwise and remove the seeds in the middle.
9. Melt the 2 tablespoons of butter and add thyme, garlic powder, salt and pepper mixing together well.
10. Place the acorn squash cut side up on a baking sheet.
11. Pour half the mixture coating the squash on one half, and the rest on the other. Use a spoon to spread evenly.
12. Bake for 25-30 minutes, until easily pierced with a fork.
13. Serve & Enjoy!

Breakfast: Summer Fruit & Nut Butter Smoothie

SERVES: 2
PREP TIME: 5 min
COOK TIME: *none

Ingredients:
1 cup frozen berries
1 banana
3 Tbsp almond butter
1 cup almond milk
1 Tbsp honey
1 tsp Chia seeds
Directions:
1. Combine all ingredients in a blender or magic bullet.
2. Blend and ready to go!
3. Serve & Enjoy!

Lunch: Chicken Salad with Bacon, Avocado and Tomatoes

SERVES: 2-3
PREP TIME: 5 min
COOK TIME: 30 min

Ingredients:
4 small pieces of chicken breast
1 bundle of Romaine Lettuce
2 tomatoes
4 slices of bacon
2 Tbsp Avocado Oil
Pepper
Salt
Cold pressed olive oil
Directions:
1. Cut the chicken breast into small pieces and add 1/2 tsp of salt and pepper.
2. Heat the oil in a pan over medium temperature.
3. Add the chicken breasts into the pan and fry until golden brown (25-30 min), mixing often.
4. Wash and cut the lettuce into bite sized pieces and place into a bowl.
5. Wash and slice the tomato and add to the salad bowl.
6. Dice avocado and add to salad bowl.
7. Place 4 slices of bacon into microwave for 4-5 minutes.
8. Chop the bacon slices into small pieces and add to the salad bowl.
9. Once chicken is cooked, add to the salad bowl.
10. Add salt, pepper and cold pressed olive oil and mix well.
11. Serve & Enjoy!

Dinner: Baked Sweet Potato

SERVES: 2
PREP TIME: 5 min
COOK TIME: 20-25 min

Ingredients:
2 sweet potatoes
Coconut oil
Nutmeg
Cinnamon

Directions:
1. Preheat the oven to 400F.
2. Wash the sweet potatoes and pierce with a fork all around the thickest part of the sweet potato.
3. Wrap in aluminum foil and cook in oven for 20-25 minutes.
4. Pierce with a fork to ensure it's cooked completely through and remove from oven.
5. Cut out a 1/2" wedge length-wise.
6. Melt 4 tablespoons coconut oil and in a bowl, mix with 2 tsp cinnamon and 2 tsp nutmeg.
7. Pour half the mixture into each potato.
8. Serve & Enjoy!

Breakfast: Banana Bread w/ Almond Butter

SERVES: 4
PREP TIME: 5 min
COOK TIME: 60 min

Ingredients:
4 ripe bananas
3 eggs
¼ cup Coconut oil
1 tsp Vanilla extract
1 cup Almond flour
½ cup Coconut flour
1 tsp Baking powder
Salt
2 tsp Cinnamon
2 Tbsp Honey
3 dates
Directions:
1. Preheat oven to 350F.
2. Using a blender or magic bullet, puree the bananas.
3. Melt ¼ cup of coconut oil and add the eggs and 1 tsp of vanilla extract together, mixing well.
4. In another bowl, add 1 cup almond flour, 1/2 cup coconut flour, 1 tsp baking powder, pinch of salt and 2 tsp cinnamon.
5. Chop the dates and add to the dry mixture.
6. Add 2 Tbsp of honey to the dry mixture and the bananas.
7. Using coconut oil, grease a loaf pan.
8. Pour the mixture into the pan and bake for 45-50 minutes.
9. Using a toothpick, insert into the loaf and make sure it comes out dry. This will indicate it's cooked all the way through!
10. Set aside for 10-15 minutes and carefully remove from the pan.
11. Serve & Enjoy!

Lunch: Beef & Broc Stir-fry

SERVES: 2-3
PREP TIME: 5 min
COOK TIME: 20-25 min

Ingredients:
2 Tbsp Avocado Oil
1 lb beef sirloin
Head of broccoli
1 Red bell pepper
2 carrots
1 green onion
2 garlic cloves
2 Tbsp sesame seeds
Coconut aminos (paleo soy sauce!)
Directions:
1. Cut the 1lb beef sirloin into strips around 2" thick.
2. Wash and cut the broccoli, red pepper, carrots and green onion.
3. Mince the garlic.
4. In a medium saucepan, heat 3 tablespoons of oil on medium-high temperature.
5. Add the beef strips and cook for 3-4 minutes, until brown.
6. Remove the beef and put on a plate on the side.
7. In the same oil, add all the cut vegetables and cook for 2-3 minutes.
8. Stir beef into the vegetables and add 2 Tbsp coconut aminos and 2 Tbsp sesame seeds.
9. Cook until all vegetables are tender and meat is fully cooked.
10. Serve & Enjoy!

Dinner: Swiss Chard & Sweet Potato Goodness

SERVES: 2-3
PREP TIME: 5 min
COOK TIME: 30 min

Ingredients:
1 bundle of Swiss chard
3 garlic cloves
2 sweet potatoes
Cold pressed olive oil
Pepper
Salt
Directions:
1. Fill a pot with water and add a dash of sea salt.
2. Bring to a boil and add diced sweet potatoes.
3. Cook until potatoes are done (about 20 minutes), should be soft and easily pierced with a fork.
4. Remove the potatoes and leave on a plate to cool.
5. Wash the Swiss chard with cold water.
6. In the same boiled water, add Swiss chard and cook for no more than 8 minutes.
7. When Swiss chard is done, using tongs take out of the boiling water and place into a serving dish.
8. Cut the yams or sweet potatoes into bite-sized pieces and add to the Swiss chard in the serving dish.
9. Mince the garlic cloves and put directly into the serving dish.
10. Add salt, pepper and pour cold pressed olive oil overtop. Mix well altogether!
11. Serve & Enjoy!

Breakfast: Veggie Patties

SERVES: 2-3
PREP TIME: 5 min
COOK TIME: 20 min

Ingredients:
2 carrots
2 celery sticks
1 zucchini
1 egg
1 Tbsp of coconut flour
1 chilli pepper
1 pepper (green or red)
1 small ginger root (if it is big, cut in half)
1 garlic clove
Pepper
Salt
2 Tbsp Avocado Oil

Directions:
1. Grate all the vegetables and put into one large bowl. Add the egg, and salt and pepper to taste.
2. Mix well together.
3. Using your hands roll out small-medium sized patties.
4. On low temperature, heat the oil in the pan. Place patties (depending on the size of the pan, 4 patties should fit at one time) and cook one side for 4-6 min.
5. Flip patties to other side and cook for 4-6 min.
6. Once first round of patties are done, repeat the process for the rest.
7. Serve & Enjoy!

Lunch: Chicken Burgers & Guacamole

SERVES: 2-3
PREP TIME: 5 min
COOK TIME: 25 min

Ingredients:
2 - 3 ripe avocados
Salt
Pepper
1 Lime, juiced
Fresh cilantro finely chopped
Pinch of chilli flakes
1 LB ground chicken
2 Tbsp fresh dill
3 chives
1 tsp oregano
2 garlic cloves
1 lemon
1/2 tsp paprika
Salt
Pepper
2 Tbsp Avocado Oil
Directions:
1. Dice ripe avocados into tiny pieces and put into a bowl.
2. Using a fork mash the avocados well. (Can also use a blender or Magic Bullet.)
3. Add a pinch of salt, tsp of pepper, juice of 1/2 lime, finely chopped cilantro and 1/2 tsp of chilli flakes.
4. Whip together well with a fork until consistency is smooth and creamy
5. In a large bowl, mix the ground chicken with finely chopped fresh dill, chives, oregano flakes, minced garlic cloves, paprika, 1 tsp salt and pepper and juice of 1 lemon.
6. Using hands make into equal sized patties.
7. Heat 3 Tbsp of oil over medium heat in a large saucepan.
8. Add 2 patties side by side, careful not to overlap, and cook for 4 minutes on each side. Repeat until all patties are cooked.
9. Place on a plate and a spoonful of guacamole on top.
10. Serve & Enjoy!

Dinner: Mexican style Salad

SERVES: 2-3
PREP TIME: 5 min
COOK TIME: 20 min

Ingredients:
1 cauliflower
1/3 cup of veggie/chicken all-natural broth or water
Garlic powder
Cayenne pepper
Fresh parsley
1 lime
½ lb lean ground pork
½ lb lean ground beef
1 Onion
1 Avocado
Salsa
2 Tbsp Avocado Oil
Salt
Pepper
Directions:
1. Grate the florets of the cauliflower into small pieces.
2. Add the grated cauliflower and broth (or water) into a pan and cook on medium temperature for about 10 minutes.
3. Add the cayenne pepper, parsley, lime, salt and pepper to the cauliflower once it's soft.
4. In a frying pan heat oil at medium temperature.
5. Dice the onion and add to the pan, along with the 1/2lb of ground pork and 1/2lb of ground beef.
6. Mix well and cook thoroughly until all red raw meat is a gray/brown colour. 7. Add the salsa and 1/2 cup of water and let simmer together for 10 minutes.
8. Dice the avocado.
9. In a bowl scoop out cauliflower rice, and top with meat mixture, sliced avocado, a tsp of fresh salsa and chopped fresh cilantro (or parsley).
10. Salt and pepper to taste.
11. Serve & Enjoy!

Breakfast: Avocado Sunny Side Up! Eggs

SERVES: 1
PREP TIME: 5 min
COOK TIME: 10 min

Ingredients:
1 avocado
2 eggs
Pepper
Salt
1 Green onion
Directions:
1. Preheat oven to 425F.
2. Slice the avocado in half and remove the pit.
3. Using a tablespoon scoop out one spoonful of avocado from the center.
4. Crack an egg directly into each avocado half.
5. Sprinkle with pepper and salt to taste.
6. Chop the green onion and sprinkle on top.
7. Bake for 15-20 minutes.
8. Serve & Enjoy!

Lunch: Mussels

SERVES: 2-3
PREP TIME: 5 min
COOK TIME: 15 min

Ingredients:
4.5 lbs of fresh mussels
10 garlic cloves
2 Tbsp Avocado Oil
Pepper
Fresh Italian parsley
*Optional – 3.5oz white wine
Directions:
1. Scrub, wash and clean mussels in water.
2. Mince garlic cloves.
3. Chop fresh parsley.
4. Heat the oil over medium heat in a large, wide-bottomed pot with a lid.
5. Add garlic and sauté until it's soft, not brown.
6. Add mussels and wine (optional) or clam juice.
7. Add pepper to taste.
8. Cover with lid and cook for 10 min or until mussels open.
9. Once mussels are opened add parsley and cook for another 1 minute (max 2min)

10. Serve & Enjoy!

Dinner: Casserole Cave Style

SERVES: 4
PREP TIME: 5 min
COOK TIME: 20 min

Ingredients:
2lb ground beef
1 packet taco seasoning
3 tsp arrowroot starch
2 Tbsp Avocado Oil
1 medium onion
3 peppers (red or green)
3 large tomatoes
Salt
Pepper
Directions:
1. Preheat oven to 350F.
2. Heat 2 Tbsp of oil over medium heat in a medium saucepan or non-stick skillet.
3. Add the beef and cook completely until all ground beef is a golden brown colour.
4. Remove the beef and add another 2 Tbsp of oil to the pan.
5. Wash and dice the peppers and chop the onions.
6. Add the vegetables to the pan and cook for 10 minutes, until onions are translucent.
7. Wash and dice the tomatoes into small pieces.
8. Add the beef and tomatoes to the pan.
9. In a small bowl, combine 1 packet of taco seasoning with arrowroot and mix together.
10. Add to the frying pan and stir everything.
11. Cook on low heat simmering for another 5-10minutes.
12. Add salt and pepper to taste.
13. Serve & Enjoy!

WEEK #3
MEAL CALENDAR

	BREAKFAST	LUNCH	DINNER
MONDAY	Pumpkin Loaf	Bacon & Tomato Quiche	Chicken & Mushroom Gravy
TUESDAY	Scrambled Eggs & Bacon	Wild Sockeye Salmon	Good Ole Meatloaf
WEDNESDAY	Summer Fruit & Nut Butter Smoothie	Lettuce Wraps	Bacon Pork Loin
THURSDAY	Paleo Oatmeal & Fruit	Kale Salad with Avocado Dressing	Cauli Rice & Green Curry
FRIDAY	Coconut Breakfast Bar	Curry Chicken Salad	Swiss Chard & Sweet Potato Goodness
SATURDAY	Apple Cinnamon Muffins	Shrimp Tacos	Chicken Alfredo & Bacon
SUNDAY	Veggie Turkey Scramble	Chorizo Chili	BBQ Pork & Veggie Skewers

WEEK#3
SHOPPING LIST

*FRUITS & VEGETABLES ALL ORGANIC AND/OR WILD
*MEATS FREE RANGE, NO ANTIBIOTICS OR HORMONES ADDED
*FISH OCEAN WISE & WILD
*Remember to always read the ingredients and check for added sugars, chemicals and MSG etc.

2 ORGANIC LEMONS
3 ORGANIC LIMES
5 AVOCADOES
1 BUNCH ORGANIC KALE
1 BUNDLE ORGANIC SWISS CHARD
1 ORGANIC CELERY STICK
1 WHOLE GARLIC
1 ORGANIC GREEN BELL PEPPER
4 ORGANIC RED BELL PEPPERS
1 ORGANIC HEAD OF LETTUCE
5 MEDIUM ONIONS
1 RED ONION
1 PACKAGE BOK CHOY
1 MEDIUM SPAGHETTI SQUASH
5 ORGANIC TOMATOES
6 ZUCCHINIS
45 ORGANIC BROWN MUSHROOMS
2 CARROT STICKS
2 JALAPENO PEPPERS
2 SWEET POTATOES
1 ORGANIC BROCCOLI
2 ORGANIC CAULIFLOWERS
1 ROMAINE LETTUCE
1 BUNDLE ORGANIC CILANTRO
1 PACKAGE ORGANIC FRESH ROSEMARY
1 BUNDLE ORGANIC SPINACH

3 ORGANIC APPLES
2 BANANAS
1 SMALL PACKAGE FRESH BERRIES (BLUEBERRY, STRAWBERRY, RASPBERRY)

2 PACKAGES FREE RANGE NO ANTIOBIOTIC EGGS (24 TOTAL)

2 CANS HEAVY COCONUT CREAM
1 CAN COCONUT MILK
1 28OZ CRUSHED TOMATOES
1 14OZ DICED TOMATOES
1 15OZ TOMATOE SAUCE
1 12OZ CAN PUMPKIN PUREE
1 SMALL JAR OF UNSWEETENED APPLESAUCE
1 500 ML ALL NATURAL VEGETABLE BROTH (NO SUGAR, NO MSG ADDED)

1 PACKAGE ALMOND FLOUR/MEAL

1 PACKAGE MSG-FREE, NO NITRATE BACON
1LB OCEAN WISE SHRIMP, PEELED AND DEVEINED
1 LARGE PIECE WILD SOCKEY SALMON
4 NO-ANTIOBIOTIC ALL NATURAL CHICKEN BREASTS
200G ORGANIC GROUND TURKEY
300G CHORIZO SAUSAGES
2LB (1KG) PORK TENDERLOIN
2 SMALL ORGANIC PORK CUTLETS
3LB ALL NATURAL GROUND BEEF
1 1/2 LB SLICED ALL NATURAL CHICKEN

100G DRIED WILD BLUEBERRIES
100G PECANS
100G PISTACHIOS
100G RAISINS
100G WALNUTS
100G PECANS
100G PUMPKIN SEEDS
100G WALNUTS
50G SUNFLOWER SEEDS
200G ALMONDS

1 BOTTLE SULFIRE-FREE ORGANIC RED WINE

WEEK #3
RECIPES

Breakfast: Pumpkin Loaf

SERVES: 4
PREP TIME: 5 min
COOK TIME: 50 min

Ingredients:
1 can pumpkin puree (12 oz)
3 eggs
2 cups almond flour
1 Tbsp vanilla extract
1 tsp baking soda
1 tsp pumpkin spice
1 tsp cinnamon
1/4 cup honey
1/4 cup coconut oil
Salt
Directions:
1. Preheat oven to 350F.
2. In a blender or magic bullet mix the pumpkin, eggs, vanilla, honey and melted coconut oil together.
3. Add the almond flour, salt, pumpkin spice, cinnamon and baking soda into the mixture.
4. Mix everything together well.
5. Grease a loaf pan well with coconut oil.
6. Pour batter into the pan and bake for 50 minutes.
7. Serve & Enjoy!

Lunch: Bacon & Tomato Quiche

SERVES: 2-3
PREP TIME: 5 min
COOK TIME: 40 min

Ingredients:
2 zucchini
1 egg
2 Tbsp coconut flour
1 Tbsp coconut oil
Salt
5 eggs
Egg whites from 3 eggs (additional)
3 Tbsp almond milk
5 bacon slices
Cauliflower head
Fresh spinach
Pepper
2 tomatoes
Directions:
1. Preheat oven to 400F.
2. Wash and grate the zucchinis.
3. Using a paper towel squeeze the zucchini to drain as much liquid as possible.
4. In a bowl, mix the grated zucchini, 1 egg, coconut flour and salt.
5. Melt the coconut oil and add to the mixture.
6. Pour mixture into a pie dish and spread evenly until the dish.
7. Bake for 8-10 minutes.
8. Remove from oven and set aside.
9. Wash and grate the cauliflower head until you fill 2/3cup of cauliflower rice. (Make sure to drain well)
10. In a bowl, add the cauliflower rice, eggs, almond milk, egg whites, salt and pepper.
11. Mix well together and pour onto crust in pie dish.
12. Wash and cut the tomatoes into slices.
13. Cut the bacon into small bite-sized chunks.
14. Add the tomato slices and bacon chunks on top.
15. Bake for 25-30 minutes, covered.
16. Remove aluminum foil cover and bake for another 5-7 minutes. Use a toothpick to check the mixture is cooked all the way through!
17. Serve & Enjoy!

Dinner: Chicken & Mushroom Gravy

SERVES: 2
PREP TIME: 5 min
COOK TIME: 20 min

Ingredients:
2 chicken breasts
10-15 brown mushrooms
1 onion
1/4 cup butter
2 1/2 cups vegetable broth
2 Tbsp coconut aminos
1/4 cup almond flour
1/2 tsp thyme
1/2 tsp sage
Salt
Pepper
Directions:
1. In a large saucepan, over medium heat melt the butter.
2. Dice the onion and wipe the mushrooms with a damp paper towel.
3. Add the onions and mushrooms to the melted butter and sauté for 1-2 minutes.
4. Add the vegetable broth and coconut aminos and stir.
5. All the while stirring, slowly add the almond flour until thickens.
6. Bring to a simmer and leave on low heat.
7. Add thyme, sage, 1 tsp salt and pepper and cook for 8-10 minutes until gravy consistency.
8. In a separate saucepan, add 3 Tbsp of oil and heat.
9. Place chicken breast directly into pan and cook 7-8 minutes on each side until cooked all the way through.
10. Place chicken breast on a plate and cover with mushroom gravy!
11. Serve & Enjoy!

Breakfast: Scrambled Eggs & Bacon

SERVES: 1-2
PREP TIME: 5 min
COOK TIME: 10 min

Ingredients:
2 eggs
Two slices of bacon
1/2 avocado
1 tomato
Salt
Pepper
Directions:
1. Place 2 slices of bacon into a frying pan at medium heat.
2. Flip after 1 minute on each side, repeating until cooked to desired crunch-factor!
3. Remove bacon from the pan and put on a plate, leaving the grease behind.
4. Crack each of the 2 eggs directly into the pan.
5. Cook the eggs for about 3 minutes, once done take out of the pan and place on a plate.
6. Wash and cut tomato into bite size pieces and add to plate.
7. Dice the avocado and add to plate.
8. Add salt and pepper to taste.
9. Serve & Enjoy!

Lunch: Wild Sockeye Salmon

SERVES: 2-3
PREP TIME: 5 min
COOK TIME: 20-25 min

Ingredients:
1 large piece of Wild Sockeye Salmon
2 Tbsp Avocado Oil
Salt
Pepper
Mustard
2 lemon wedges
Directions:
1. Heat the oven to 400F.
2. Grease a baking sheet with oil.
3. Place salmon on baking sheet and rub with oil.
4. With a teaspoon, cover top of salmon facing up with mustard.
5. Add salt and pepper and juice of 2 lemon wedges.
6. Place in oven and cook uncovered for 20 - 25 minutes.
7. Check every 10 min.
8. When Salmon flakes easily with fork and the top is lightly brown, it's done.
9. Allow to sit for 2 minutes, then cut into 3-4 pieces and serve (pairs nicely with any salad)
10. Serve & Enjoy!

Dinner: Good Ole Meatloaf
SERVES: 2-3
PREP TIME: 5 min
COOK TIME: 60 min

Ingredients:
1lb ground beef
2 cups almond flour
1 can coconut milk
2 garlic cloves
2 carrots
1 medium onion
1 zucchini
1 egg
Parsley flakes
Oregano flakes
Chilli flakes
Salt
Pepper
2 Tbsp Avocado Oil
Directions:
1. Preheat Oven to 350F.
2. In a medium bowl, add 1/3 cup coconut milk and 2 cups almond flour and mix well.
3. In a large saucepan, heat 3 tablespoons of oil over medium heat.
4. Dice ½ an onion.
5. Wash and chop zucchini and carrots.
6. Mince the garlic.
7. In the saucepan, add carrots, onion, zucchini and garlic for 5-7 minutes.
8. Remove sautéed vegetables from heat and put aside.
9. Add the vegetables into the bowl of coconut milk and almond flour.
10. Add the ground beef, egg, 1 tsp each of parsley, oregano, chilli flakes, salt and pepper and mix well.
11. Grease a loaf pan and pour mixture into it, spreading evenly.
12. Cook for 45-50 minutes in the oven.
13. Serve & Enjoy!

Breakfast: Summer Fruit & Nut Butter Smoothie
SERVES: 1-2
PREP TIME: 5 min
COOK TIME: *none

Ingredients:
1 cup frozen berries
1 banana
3 Tbsp almond butter
1 cup almond milk
1 Tbsp honey
1 tsp chia seeds
Directions:
1. Combine all ingredients in a blender or magic bullet.
2. Blend and its ready to go!
3. Serve & Enjoy!

Lunch: Lettuce Wraps

SERVES: 2-3
PREP TIME: 5 min
COOK TIME: 20 min

Ingredients:
Romaine lettuce
1 avocado
1 lemon
1 chicken breast
1 tomato
1 red onion
1 red pepper (orange or green OK)
Salt
Pepper
2 Tbsp Avocado Oil
Directions:
1. In a small saucepan, heat 3 Tbsp of oil over medium temperature.
2. Add the chicken breast to hot oil and cook 5-7 minutes on each side, until chicken is thoroughly cooked.
3. Let cool to the side.
4. Wash romaine lettuce leaves and put 5 aside.
5. Wash and cut the tomato and pepper.
6. Dice 1/3 cup red onion.
7. Take the chicken breast and cut into small cubes.
8. Slice the avocado in half and put entire avocado into a bowl, mashing it with a fork.
9. Add the juice of 1 lemon, 1 tsp salt and pepper to the avocado and mix.
10. Add the red onion, tomato, pepper and chicken breast into the avocado bowl and mix well.
11. Using a large spoon, dish out 2 tablespoons of the mixture into each lettuce leaf.
12. Serve & Enjoy!

Dinner: Bacon Pork Loin

SERVES: 2-3
PREP TIME: 10 min
COOK TIME: 30 min

Ingredients:
2 eggs
1/2 cup almond flour
Fresh rosemary
1 tsp onion powder
1 tsp sea salt
2 pounds (1 kg) pork tenderloin
6 slices of bacon
Directions:
1. Heat oven to 425F.
2. Whisk the eggs together in a big bowl.
3. On a plate, mix together almond flour, onion powder and sea salt.
4. Take the pork tenderloin and dip generously into the eggs, then directly coat with the almond flour spice mixture.
5. Using ALL 6 bacon slices, wrap around the pork covering as much as possible.
6. Tuck a stem of fresh rosemary between the bacon slice and pork tenderloin.
7. Bake in the oven for 25-30 minutes.
8. Serve while still hot.
9. Serve & Enjoy!

Breakfast: Paleo Oatmeal & Fruit

SERVES: 2
PREP TIME: 5 min
COOK TIME: 5 min

Ingredients:
2 egg whites
1/2 cup almond milk
1 Tbsp ground flax
1 tsp cinnamon
1/2 banana
Almond butter
Fresh berries (blue, rasp, straw etc)
Directions:
1. Mash 1/2 a banana and put into a small saucepan.
2. Add the remaining ingredients and stir.
3. On medium heat, constantly stirring cook for 3-5 minutes until starts to become creamy.
4. Top with a spoonful of almond butter and 3 Tbsp of berries (blueberries, strawberries, raspberries etc.)
5. Serve & Enjoy!

Lunch: Kale Salad with Avocado Dressing
SERVES: 2-3
PREP TIME: 10 min
COOK TIME: *none

Ingredients:
1 bunch of kale
1 apple
1/2 cup walnuts
1 Tbsp olive oil
1 lemon
1 avocado
1/4 cup water
1 lime
1 Tbsp maple syrup
1 tsp cumin
2 Tbsp coriander leaves
Salt
Pepper
Directions:
1. Wash the kale and remove the stalks.
2. Tear into bite sized chunks into a large bowl and add olive oil and juice of 1/2 lemon and mix well.
3. Chop 1/2 cup of walnuts and add to mixture.
4. Wash and cut the apple into slices, adding to mixture.
5. In a blender or magic bullet, add 1 avocado, 1/4 cup water, juice of 1 lime, 1 Tbsp maple syrup 1 tsp cumin, 3 Tbsp coriander leaves and 1 tsp of salt and pepper.
6. Blend well until a completely smooth texture.
7. Pour the dressing over the salad and mix well.
8. Serve & Enjoy!

Dinner: Cauli Rice & Green Curry

SERVES: 2-3
PREP TIME: 5 min
COOK TIME: 20 min

Ingredients:
Head of cauliflower
1/3 cup water
Cayenne pepper

Parsley
Salt
Pepper
Green curry paste (preservative & sugar-free)
1 LB chicken slices
2 cups coconut cream
1 Tbsp fish sauce
1 lime
Broccoli head
1 zucchini
1 pack bok choy
Coconut oil
Directions:
1. Grate the florets of the cauliflower into small pieces.
2. Add the grated cauliflower into a pan filled with 1/2 cup water and cook on medium temperature for about 10 minutes.
3. Add the cayenne pepper, parsley, salt and pepper to the cauliflower once it's soft.
4. In a large saucepan, over medium heat add 3 Tbsp coconut oil.
5. Add 3 Tbsp green curry paste and cook for 2-3 minutes.
6. Add the sliced chicken slices and cook until golden brown 5-7 minutes, stirring often.
7. Wash and cut vegetables into bite-sized pieces.
8. Add the coconut cream, fish sauce and vegetables.
9. Cook for 7-10 minutes until vegetables are fully cooked.
10. Leave on the side for 5 minutes letting all the flavours combine.
11. Dish out cauliflower rice and top with chicken green curry.
12. Serve & Enjoy!

Breakfast: Coconut Breakfast Bar

SERVES: 2-3
PREP TIME: 5 min
COOK TIME: 60 min in the fridge (no cooking)

Ingredients:
1 1/2 cups shredded coconut
3/4 cup whole almonds
1/2 cup pistachios
1/2 cup dried blueberries
1/3 cup walnuts
1/3 cup pumpkin seeds
1/3 cup pecans
1/3 cup hemp seeds
1/4 cup sunflower seeds
1/3 cup honey
1/4 cup apple sauce (unsweetened!)
1 cup almond butter
Directions:
1. Line a baking pan (best is 8'x8') with parchment paper.
2. In a large bowl, mix the shredded coconut, almonds, pistachios, dried blueberries, walnuts, pumpkin seeds, pecans, hemp seeds and sunflower seeds altogether.
3. Add the honey and applesauce and mix well.
4. Add the cup of almond butter to the mixture and mix very well.
5. Pour the mixture into the pan and distribute evenly.
6. Leave in the freezer for at least 1 hour.
7. Using a sharp knife, cut into squares or rectangles for your choice of serving size!
8. Serve & Enjoy!

Lunch: Curry Chicken Salad

SERVES: 2-3
PREP TIME: 5 min
COOK TIME: 20 min

Ingredients:
1 chicken breast
1 celery stick
1 red apple
1/2 cup pecans
1/2 cup raisins
1/4 cup coconut cream
2 Tbsp curry paste
Salt
Pepper
Cayenne pepper
2 Tbsp Avocado Oil
Directions:
1. In a medium saucepan, heat 2 Tbsp of oil over medium temperature.
2. Grill the chicken breast, 5-6 minutes on each side ensuring it's cooked all the way through.
3. Slice the chicken breast into bite sized pieces and put aside.
4. Wash and dice the celery stick into very small pieces.
5. Wash and cut 1/2 a red apple into very small pieces.
6. Chop the pecans with a knife into small pieces.
7. In a medium bowl add the chicken breast pieces, diced celery, red apple pieces and pecans.
8. Add the raisins, 1 tsp of cayenne pepper, salt and pepper.
9. In a small bowl, combine 1/4 cup coconut cream with 2 Tbsp curry paste.
10. Mix the two together well and add bowl with all other ingredients.
11. Stir well together coating with curry sauce.
12. Serve & Enjoy!

Dinner: Swiss Chard & Sweet Potato Goodness
SERVES: 2-3
PREP TIME: 5 min
COOK TIME: 20-25 min

Ingredients:
1 bundle of Swiss chard
3 garlic cloves
2 sweet potatoes
Cold pressed olive oil
Pepper
Salt
Directions:
1. Fill a pot with water and add a dash of sea salt.
2. Bring to a boil and add diced yams or sweet potatoes.
3. Cook until potatoes are done (about 20 minutes), should be soft and easily pierced with a fork.
4. Remove the potatoes and leave on a plate to cool.
5. Wash the Swiss chard with cold water.
6. In the same boiled water, add Swiss chard and cook for no more than 8 minutes.
7. When Swiss chard is done, using tongs take out of the boiling water and place into a serving dish.
8. Cut the yams or sweet potatoes into bite-sized pieces and add to the Swiss chard in the serving dish.
9. Mince the garlic cloves and put directly into the serving dish.
10. Add salt, pepper and pour cold pressed olive oil overtop. Mix well together!
11. Serve & Enjoy!

Breakfast: Apple Cinnamon Muffins
SERVES: 2-3
PREP TIME: 5 min
COOK TIME: 10-15 min

Ingredients:
2 1/4 cups almond flour
Pinch sea salt
1/2 tsp baking soda
1 tsp cinnamon
1/4 tsp nutmeg
1 apple (sour green apples)
2 eggs
1/3 cup coconut oil
1/4 cup honey or maple syrup
Directions:
1. Preheat the oven to 375F.
2. Wash and dice the apple.
3. In a bowl, mix all the dry ingredients together. Add the diced apple.
4. Melt the coconut oil and add honey or maple syrup, mixing well.
5. Add eggs to the wet mixture and mix.
6. Add the wet mixture to all the dry ingredients and mix well.
7. Using coconut oil, grease the tray.
8. With a large tablespoon, fill the muffin cups with the mixture to 1/2" under the top
9. Bake for 10-15 minutes, until tops are a golden brown colour. You can always check with a toothpick, by inserting into the muffin - if comes out dry they're done! :)
10. Serve & Enjoy!

Lunch: Shrimp Tacos

SERVES: 2-3
PREP TIME: 10 min
COOK TIME: 20 min

Ingredients:
6 egg whites
1/4 cup coconut flour
1/4 cup almond milk
Salt
1 tsp chilli powder
1 tsp cumin
2 Tbsp Avocado Oil
1 tsp chilli powder
Salt
1 lb medium shrimp
1 avocado
1 lettuce head
Fresh cilantro
1 lime
Directions:
1. Combine egg whites, coconut flour, almond milk, salt and chilli powder and mix well in a large bowl.
2. In a large skillet or saucepan, heat 1 Tbsp of oil over medium heat.
3. Pour 3 Tbsp of batter into the pan and spread the batter out like a crepe.
4. Cook 2-3 minutes, or until taco loosens easily in the pan and flip carefully.
5. Repeat with remaining batter.
6. In a medium bowl, toss the shrimp with 1 tsp chilli powder, salt and pepper coating well.
7. In a medium saucepan, heat 1 Tbsp of oil over medium heat.
8. Add the shrimp and cook for 3-4 minutes until shrimp are cooked through.
9. Dice the avocado and chop the fresh cilantro.
10. Shred the lettuce.
11. In a taco shell, scoop out 4 Tbsp shrimp mixture, 1 Tbsp of avocado, add shredded lettuce and squeeze lime juice on top.
12. Serve & Enjoy!

Dinner: Chicken Alfredo + Bacon

SERVES: 2-3
PREP TIME: 5 min
COOK TIME: 30 min

Ingredients:
½ LB chicken slices
1 cup heavy coconut cream
2 Tbsp butter
4 tsp Arrowroot Powder
1 tsp garlic powder
Salt
Pepper
2 slices of bacon
1 spaghetti squash
2 Tbsp Avocado Oil
Directions:
1. In a medium saucepan, add the coconut cream, butter, arrowroot powder, garlic powder and 1 tsp salt and pepper.
2. Heat over medium temperature carefully stirring the ENTIRE time with a whisk until everything thickens.
3. In a separate saucepan, add 2 slices of bacon on medium heat and cook until crispy for 4-5 minutes.
4. Remove the bacon from the pan and leave the grease. Cut the slices of bacon into small 1" pieces.
5. Add the chicken slices and cook covered for 4-5 minutes, and then stir.
6. Cook chicken for another 3-4 minutes until cooked all the way through.
7. Cut the spaghetti squash lengthwise and remove all seeds from the middle.
8. Put 1/2inch of water into a microwaveable plate, and place 1 half of the cut squash face down.
9. Microwave for 6-8 minutes.
10. Leave to sit for a few minutes then use a fork to separate out the spaghetti strands.
11. Repeat with the remaining spaghetti squash.
12. Add the spaghetti squash, bacon pieces and chicken to the Alfredo mixture.
13. Mix well.
14. Serve & Enjoy!

Breakfast: Veggie Turkey Scramble

SERVES: 2
PREP TIME: 5 min
COOK TIME: 20 min

Ingredients:
3 eggs
1/4 cup ground turkey
1 zucchini
1 tomato
1 medium onion
1 yellow or red pepper
1 avocado
Salt
Pepper
1 garlic clove
2 Tbsp Avocado Oil
Directions:
1. In a medium saucepan, heat 2 Tbsp of oil over medium heat.
2. Add the ground turkey meat and cook for 7-10 minutes until all meat is thoroughly cooked.
3. In another frying pan, heat 2 Tbsp of oil over medium heat.
4. Add ¼ cup zucchini sliced 1/2 of the onion, 1/4 of chopped pepper and cook for 3-4 minutes.
5. In a bowl, whisk together the eggs.
6. Pour the eggs over the veggies and stir frequently as they scrambled.
7. Add the ground turkey and scramble all together.
8. Wash and cut the tomato into slices.
9. Dice the avocado.
10. Plate the turkey scramble and top with tomato slices, avocado and salt and pepper to taste.
11. Serve & Enjoy!

Lunch: Chorizo Chilli
SERVES: 2-3
PREP TIME: 5 min
COOK TIME: 40 min

Ingredients:
1 LB ground beef
¾ LB chorizo sausage
1 medium onion
2 red peppers
15-20 brown mushrooms
4 garlic cloves
2 jalapeno peppers
1 can tomato sauce (15oz)
1 can crushed tomatoes (28oz)
1 can diced tomatoes (14oz)
Red wine (optional)
Chilli flakes
Paprika
Dried oregano
Dried basil
Cayenne pepper
Onion powder
Salt
Pepper
2 Tbsp Avocado Oil
Directions:
1. In a large saucepan heat 3 Tbsp of oil at low-med temperature
2. Add the ground beef and sliced chorizo sausage and cook for 5-7 minutes until beef is brown and completely cooked.
3. Wash the red peppers and cut into small pieces.
4. Pat dry with a damp paper towel all the brown mushrooms. Cut into squares.
5. Finely chop the jalapeno peppers, dice onion and mince garlic.
6. Add the peppers, mushrooms, jalapeno peppers, garlic into the meat and stir for 1-2 minutes.
7. Add the tomato sauce, crushed tomatoes and diced tomatoes with 1 cup of water and stir well.
8. Add a splash of red wine (optional).
9. Add 1 tsp each of the chilli flakes, paprika, oregano, basil, cayenne pepper, onion powder, salt and pepper.

10. Stir altogether and bring to a boil.

11. Reduce to medium temperature and cook for 30-35 minutes, stirring at the 15minute mark.

12. Serve & Enjoy!

Dinner: BBQ Pork & Veggie skewers

SERVES: 2-3
PREP TIME: 5 min
COOK TIME: 20 min

Ingredients:
2 pork cutlets
Olive oil
Salt
Pepper
1 zucchini
15-20 brown mushrooms
1 medium onion
2 red peppers
1 green pepper
Chilli flakes
Directions:
1. Rub salt and pepper onto pork cutlets.
2. Pour olive oil on both sides of cutlets and rub in well.
3. Light the BBQ and heat up to a medium flame.
4. Put the pork cutlets on the BBQ.
5. Cook 12 min on each side, checking every 5 min. Add tsp of olive oil as needed during cooking.
6. Wash and cut the zucchini, red and green peppers.
7. With a damp paper towel, wipe the tops of the mushrooms clean.
8. Cut the onion, red and green peppers into squares.
9. Cut the mushrooms in half.
10. Slice the zucchini into 1/2" thick slices.
11. Place all vegetables into a large bowl, add 3 Tbsp of olive oil, salt, pepper and chilli flakes and mix well.
12. Using metal or wood skewers start to layer the vegetables zucchini, red pepper, mushroom, green pepper, onion and repeat.
13. Leave some space between each vegetable and 1/2" space on each end.

14. Place on BBQ and cook for 5-10 minutes, flipping on each side every 2-3 minutes.

15. Serve & Enjoy!

WEEK #4
MEAL CALENDAR

	BREAKFAST	LUNCH	DINNER
MONDAY	Eggs & Bacon Muffins	Zucchini Pad Thai	Chicken & Mushroom Gravy
TUESDAY	Coconut Breakfast Bar	Bacon Asparagus Wrap with Roasted Vegetables	Baked Sweet Potato
WEDNESDAY	Scrambled Eggs & Bacon	Bacon & Tomato Quiche	Spaghetti & Meat Sauce Paleo Style
THURSDAY	Coconut Blueberry Pancakes	Turkey Patties	Paleo Pizza
FRIDAY	Paleo Granola & Fruit	*Leftover* Paleo Pizza	Shrimp Salad
SATURDAY	Avocado Sunny Side UP! Eggs	Octopus & Crab Salad	Paleo Enchiladas
SUNDAY	Paleo Pancakes	Paleo style Fajitas	Meat & Potato Bake

WEEK#4
RECIPES

Breakfast: Egg & Bacon Muffins
SERVES: 2
PREP TIME: 5 min
COOK TIME: 15 min

Ingredients:
4 slices of bacon
4 eggs
3 chives (or green onion)
Salt
Pepper
2 Tbsp Avocado Oil

Directions:
1. Put 4 slices of bacon into a medium saucepan over low-med heat and cook for 2-3 minutes until cooked, but still soft and not crispy.
2. Put aside.
3. Preheat oven to 375F.
4. Grease muffin tray with oil.
5. Take 1 slice of bacon and wrap the inside of the muffin cup create a circle.
6. Crack an egg directly into each bacon lined muffin cup.
7. Wash and chop the chives.
8. Sprinkle each egg with 1 tsp salt, pepper and 1 tsp chives.
9. Cook for 12-15 minutes, until the egg center are set.
10. Serve & Enjoy!

Lunch: Zucchini Pad Thai
SERVES: 2-3
PREP TIME: 5 min
COOK TIME: 20 min

Ingredients:
1/4 cup coconut or avocado oil
3 zucchinis
1 medium onion
1 garlic clove
1 tablespoon apple cider vinegar
1 ginger root
1 Tbsp Almond butter
1 Tbsp Chilli paste
1 Tbsp Fish sauce
1 lime, juiced
Salt
Pepper

Directions:
1. Slice the zucchinis very thinly length-wise and put into a bowl. (Or use a mandolin.)
2. Chop the onion and mince the garlic.
3. Peel and cut up 1"x1" of the ginger root, cutting into small pieces.
4. In a medium frying pan, heat 2 Tbsp of oil over medium temperature.
5. Add the onion, garlic and ginger and cook 3-5 minutes until soft.
6. Add 1 tablespoon of fish sauce, chilli past, apple cider vinegar, juice of 1 lime, almond butter and a pinch of salt.
7. Mix everything together well in the pan and cook for 5 minutes.
8. Add the zucchini noodles to the pan and stir in well, cooking for another 10 minutes.
9. Serve & Enjoy!

Dinner: Chicken & Mushroom Gravy
SERVES: 2
PREP TIME: 5 min
COOK TIME: 20 min

Ingredients:
2 chicken breasts
10-15 brown mushrooms
1 onion
1/4 cup butter
2 1/2 cups vegetable broth
2 Tbsp coconut aminos
1/4 cup almond flour
1/2 tsp thyme
1/2 tsp sage
Salt
Pepper

Directions:
1. In a large saucepan, over medium heat melt the butter.
2. Dice the onion and wipe the mushrooms with a damp paper towel.
3. Add the onions and mushrooms to the melted butter and sauté for 1-2 minutes.
4. Add the vegetable broth and coconut aminos and stir.
5. All the while stirring, slowly add the almond flour until thickens.
6. Bring to a simmer and leave on low heat.
7. Add thyme, sage, 1 tsp salt and pepper and cook for 8-10 minutes until gravy consistency.
8. In a separate saucepan, add 3 Tbsp of oil and heat.
9. Place chicken breast directly into pan and cook 7-8 minutes on each side until cooked all the way through.
10. Place chicken breast on a plate and cover with mushroom gravy!
11. Serve & Enjoy!

Breakfast: Coconut Breakfast Bar
SERVES: 4
PREP TIME: 5 min
COOK TIME: 60 min (fridge time, no cooking)

Ingredients:
1 1/2 cups shredded coconut
3/4 cup whole almonds
1/2 cup pistachios
1/2 cup dried blueberries
1/3 cup walnuts
1/3 cup pumpkin seeds
1/3 cup pecans
1/3 cup hemp seeds
1/4 cup sunflower seeds
1/3 cup honey
1/4 cup apple sauce (unsweetened!)
1 cup almond butter

Directions:
1. Line a baking pan (best is 8'x8') with parchment paper.
2. In a large bowl, mix the shredded coconut, almonds, pistachios, dried blueberries, walnuts, pumpkin seeds, pecans, hemp seeds and sunflower seeds altogether.
3. Add the honey and applesauce and mix well.
4. Add the cup of almond butter to the mixture and mix very well.
5. Pour the mixture into the pan and distribute evenly.
6. Leave in the freezer for at least 1 hour.
7. Using a sharp knife, cut into squares or rectangles for your choice of serving size!
8. Serve & Enjoy!

Lunch: Bacon Asparagus Wrap w/ Roasted Vegetables
SERVES: 2-3
PREP TIME: 5 min
COOK TIME: 35 min

Ingredients:
1 yam
1 sweet potato
2 beets
Medium onion
1 bunch of asparagus
5 slices of bacon
Salt
Pepper
Chilli flakes
Dried oregano
2 Tbsp Avocado Oil

Directions:
1. Preheat oven to 425F.
2. Wash yam, sweet potato, and beets.
3. Using a sharp knife, chop the yam, sweet potato and beets into bite-sized chunks. Try to keep them all consistent size so they cook evenly!
4. Cut the onion into square sized chunks.
5. Add 3 tablespoons of oil (if coconut, melt first!) and 1 tsp of salt, pepper and chilli flakes.
6. Mix well together in a large bowl coating all the vegetables.
7. Put into a baking dish, spreading evenly and cover with aluminum foil.
8. Cook for 25-30 minutes, and check by piercing with a fork. The fork should easily pierce any of the vegetables.
9. Remove foil, and cook for another 5 minutes.
10. Wash the asparagus stalks, and cut the 1/4" of the stalk bottom off piercing little Xs on each bottom.
11. Cut each bacon slices into 3 equal sized pieces.
12. Use each of the now, 15 bacon pieces to wrap around a stalk of asparagus diagonally.
13. When vegetables are done, remove and set aside, lowering the oven temperature to 400F.
14. Put the bacon wrapped asparagus on a baking dish placing side by side, careful not to overlap any of the pieces.
15. Cook in the oven for 5 minutes, then remove and flip.

16. Cook for another 5-7 minutes until bacon is cooked and asparagus is easily pierced with a fork.

17. Serve & Enjoy!

Dinner: Baked Sweet Potato
SERVES: 2
PREP TIME: 5 min
COOK TIME: 30 min

Ingredients:
2 sweet potatoes
Coconut oil
Nutmeg
Cinnamon

Directions:
1. Preheat the oven to 400F.
2. Wash the sweet potatoes and pierce with a fork all around the thickest part of the sweet potato.
3. Wrap in aluminum foil and cook in oven for 20-25 minutes.
4. Pierce with a fork to ensure it's cooked completely through and remove from oven.
5. Cut out a 1/2" wedge length-wise.
6. Melt 4 tablespoons coconut oil and in a bowl, mix with 2 tsp cinnamon and 2 tsp nutmeg.
7. Pour half the mixture into each potato.
8. Serve & Enjoy!

Breakfast: Scrambled Eggs & Bacon
SERVES: 1
PREP TIME: 5 min
COOK TIME: 5 min

Ingredients:
2 eggs
Two slices of bacon
1/2 avocado
1 tomato
Salt
Pepper

Directions:
1. Place 2 slices of bacon into a frying pan at medium heat.
2. Flip after 1 minute on each side, repeating until cooked to desired crunch-factor!
3. Remove bacon from the pan and put on a plate, leaving the grease behind.
4. Crack each of the 2 eggs directly into the pan.
5. Cook the eggs for about 3 minutes, once done take out of the pan and place on a plate.
6. Wash and cut tomato into bite size pieces and add to plate.
7. Dice the avocado and add to plate. Add salt and pepper to taste.
8. Serve & Enjoy!

Lunch: Bacon & Tomato Quiche
SERVES: 2-3
PREP TIME: 5 min
COOK TIME: 40 min

Ingredients:
2 zucchini
1 egg
2 Tbsp coconut flour
1 Tbsp coconut oil
Salt
5 eggs
Egg whites from 3 eggs (additional)
3 Tbsp almond milk
5 bacon slices
Cauliflower head
Fresh spinach
Pepper
2 tomatoes

Directions:
1. Preheat oven to 400F.
2. Wash and grate the zucchinis.
3. Using a paper towel squeeze the zucchini to drain as much liquid as possible.
4. In a bowl, mix the grated zucchini, 1 egg, coconut flour and salt.
5. Melt the coconut oil and add to the mixture.
6. Pour mixture into a pie dish and spread evenly until the dish.
7. Bake for 8-10 minutes.
8. Remove from oven and set aside.
9. Wash and grate the cauliflower head until you fill 2/3cup of cauliflower rice. (Make sure to drain well)
10. In a bowl, add the cauliflower rice, eggs, almond milk, egg whites, salt and pepper.
11. Mix well together and pour onto crust in pie dish.
12. Wash and cut the tomatoes into slices.
13. Cut the bacon into small bite-sized chunks.
14. Add the tomato slices and bacon chunks on top.
15. Bake for 25-30 minutes, covered.
16. Remove aluminum foil cover and bake for another 5-7 minutes.

Use a toothpick to check the mixture is cooked all the way through!
    17. Serve & Enjoy!

Dinner: Spaghetti & Meat Sauce Paleo style
SERVES: 2-3
PREP TIME: 5 min
COOK TIME: 45 min

Ingredients:
1 spaghetti squash
1 1/2 lb ground beef
1 medium onion
10-12 brown mushrooms
1 green pepper
1 red pepper
1 can crushed tomatoes (14.5 oz)
1 can diced tomatoes (8oz)
Fresh basil
Oregano flakes
Dried thyme
Chilli flakes
Salt
Pepper
2 Tbsp Avocado Oil

Directions:
1. Preheat oven to 400F.
2. Cut the spaghetti squash in half and scoop out the seeds and middle.
3. In a baking dish, pour 1" of water, and place the spaghetti squash halves cut sides down.
4. Bake for 30-40 minutes.
5. In a medium saucepan, heat 2 Tbsp of oil over medium heat.
6. Add the ground beef and diced onions and sauté until beef is fully cooked and a golden brown colour.
7. Put beef aside and drain any remaining liquids in pan.
8. In same pan, heat another 1 Tbsp of oil and add mushrooms, zucchini, green and red pepper, both cans of tomatoes, chopped basil, 1 tsp of oregano and thyme.
9. Bring to a boil over medium heat and leave to simmer for 10 minutes.
10. Add the ground beef and onions back in and simmer on low heat.

11. When squash is done, using a fork separate out the strands and put into a bowl.

12. Dish out spaghetti squash and top with ground beef tomato mixture.

13. Add salt and pepper to taste.

14. Serve & Enjoy!

Breakfast: Coconut Blueberry Pancakes
SERVES: 2-3
PREP TIME: 5 min
COOK TIME: 20 min

Ingredients:
4 eggs
1 cup almond milk
2 Tbsp honey
1 tsp vanilla extract
1/2 cup coconut flour
1 tsp baking soda
Salt
1 cup blueberries
2 Tbsp Avocado Oil

Directions:
1. In a medium sized bowl, whisk the eggs, milk, honey and vanilla together.
2. In a separate bowl, add the coconut flour, baking soda, and salt together.
3. Add the wet mixture to all the dry ingredients and stir in the blueberries.
4. In a medium saucepan, heat 3 Tbsp of oil over medium heat.
5. Pour batter into pan over hot oil, usually 2 will fit side by side.
6. Once bubbles start to appear on the top of the pancake, 2 minutes or so, flip to other side until golden brown.
7. Repeat with the remaining batter until all the pancakes are cooked.
8. You can top with banana slices, almond butter or maple syrup!
9. Serve & Enjoy!

Lunch: Turkey Patties
SERVES: 2-3
PREP TIME: 10 min
COOK TIME: 40 min

Ingredients:
7oz ground turkey
1 medium onion
2 garlic cloves
400g (14 oz) tomato puree
1 egg
1 tsp hemp seeds (optional)
2 Tbsp 2 Tbsp Avocado Oil
Italian parsley
Chilli flakes
Salt
Pepper
2 oz of water

Directions:
1. Chop onion into small pieces.
2. Mince the garlic.
3. Combine the ground turkey meat with onion, garlic, egg, hemp seeds, and teaspoon of chilli flakes, salt and pepper into one bowl.
4. Mix well.
5. Leave in the fridge for 20 minutes.
6. Remove from fridge and make into patties.
7. Heat the oil over medium heat in a frying pan.
8. Once oil is hot, place the Pattie and cook 4 minutes/side.
9. Turn to low temperature and add the tomato puree (optional).
10. Cook another 3 minutes. Top with fresh Italian parsley.
11. Serve & Enjoy!

Dinner: Paleo Pizza
SERVES: 2-3
PREP TIME: 5 min
COOK TIME: 40 min

Ingredients:
1 large head of cauliflower
2 eggs
1 ½ cups tomato sauce
Zucchini
2 Green peppers
1 red or orange pepper
8-10 green olives (optional)
Dried Oregano
Salt
Pepper

Directions:
1. In a large saucepan bring 3L of water to a boil over medium heat.
2. Wash the head of cauliflower and cut off all green stems.
3. Add the head of cauliflower to the boiling water and cook for 7-8 minutes.
4. Drain EXTREMELY well. The more drained and moisture removed from the cauliflower the better the quality of your pizza crust!
5. Cut into small florets and in a food processor or using a grater make the cauliflower into a rice-like texture.
6. In a bowl, add 2 eggs, salt and pepper and mix altogether well.
7. On a pizza pan, pour out your pizza 'crust'.
8. Heat oven to 400F, and bake pizza 'crust' for 20min in the oven until starts to turn slightly brown.
9. Wash and cut the peppers and zucchini.
10. Cover pizza 'crust' with tomato sauce, spread evenly, and add zucchini and peppers as toppings.
11. Add olives and top with dried oregano.
12. Put back in the oven and bake for another 10 minutes.
13. Serve & Enjoy!

Breakfast: Paleo Granola & Fruit
SERVES: 2
PREP TIME: 10 min
COOK TIME: *none

Ingredients:
1/4 cup almonds
1/4 cup cashews
1/2 cup hazelnuts
1/3 cup dried fruit (blueberries, cranberries etc)
1 Tbsp pumpkin seeds
1 Tbsp coconut flakes
1 Tbsp honey
1 orange
1 tsp chia
1 apple or peach
1 banana
Almond milk

Directions:
1. In a blender or magic bullet, combine almonds, cashews and hazelnuts.
2. Mix for 30 seconds until small pieces but before start to butter.
3. Put into a bowl and add the dried fruit, pumpkin seeds, coconut flakes.
4. Squeeze juice of 1 orange and add to the bowl.
5. Add honey, chia and slice apple (or peach) and banana and add to the bowl.
6. Fill bowl with almond milk like you would with a bowl of cereal!
7. Serve & Enjoy!

Lunch: **last night's leftover Paleo Pizza!

Dinner: Shrimp Salad
SERVES: 2-3
PREP TIME: 5 min
COOK TIME: 20 min

Ingredients:
1-1 LB package of frozen wild shrimp
1 avocado
1 cup arugula salad
2 tomatoes
2 Tbsp Avocado Oil
Pepper
Salt

Directions:
1. Heat the oil in a frying pan over low to medium temperature.
2. Remove shrimp from package and in a bowl, run cold water over top for 3-5minutes.
3. Add the shrimp to the frying pan and cook for 10-15minutes at medium temperature, stirring frequently.
4. In a salad bowl, add arugula salad pieces.
5. Cut up the tomatoes and add to the salad bowl.
6. Dice the avocado and add to the salad bowl.
7. Add salt, pepper and cold pressed olive oil to taste.
8. Add the shrimp and mix altogether well.
9. Serve & Enjoy!

Breakfast: Avocado Sunny Side Up! Eggs
SERVES: 2
PREP TIME: 5 min
COOK TIME: 20 min

Ingredients:
1 avocado
2 eggs
Pepper
Salt
Green onion

Directions:
1. Preheat oven to 425F.
2. Slice the avocado in half and remove the pit.
3. Using a tablespoon scoop out one spoonful of avocado from the center.
4. Crack an egg directly into each avocado half.
5. Sprinkle with pepper and salt to taste.
6. Chop the green onion and sprinkle on top.
7. Bake for 15-20 minutes.
8. Serve & Enjoy!

Lunch: Octopus & Crab Salad
SERVES: 2-3
PREP TIME: 5 min
COOK TIME: 2 hr

Ingredients:
1 LB package of frozen octopus
1 lb package of frozen crab
1 package of baby arugula salad
Jar of capers
2 tomatoes
2 lemons
1/4 cup of Italian parsley
2 garlic cloves
Olive oil
Salt
Pepper

Directions:
1. Fill a pot with water and sprinkle a dash of sea salt.
2. Put octopus meat into the pot and bring to a boil over medium temperature.
3. Allow to cook for 90 - 120 min, at medium temperature.
4. When the octopus is cooked, remove and allow cooling.
5. Remove the skin of the octopus meat.
6. Cut into small bite-sized pieces & put into a serving dish.
7. Cut the crab into small pieces.
8. In a frying pan over medium heat, add oil and once heated, add crab to cook.
9. Cook for 10 minutes and put into a serving dish when done.
10. Mince garlic cloves and add to serving dish.
11. Wash and cut tomatoes into bite-sized pieces, add directly to serving dish.
12. Finely chop Italian parsley and add to serving dish.
13. Add ½ package of arugula salad to serving dish.
14. Add 2 tablespoons of capers.
15. Add salt and pepper to taste.
16. Add the juice of two lemons to serving dish.
17. Add 2 tablespoons (3oz) of cold pressed olive oil to serving dish.
18. Stir all the salad contents well together in the serving dish.
19. Keep in the fridge for 30 minutes and serve cold.
20. Serve & Enjoy!

Dinner: Paleo Enchiladas
SERVES: 2-3
PREP TIME: 5 min
COOK TIME: 20 min

Ingredients:
1 Tbsp coconut flour
4 egg whites
1 tsp baking powder
Coconut oil
1 pepper (red or green)
2 garlic cloves
1 medium onion
1 lb chicken
2 tsp cumin
2 tsp chilli powder
3 cups enchilada sauce or tomato base sauce

Directions:
1. In a medium bowl whisk coconut flour, egg whites 1/4 cup water and baking soda together.
2. Heat 1 Tbsp of oil over medium temperature in a saucepan.
3. Pour 3 Tbsp of batter into the pan and spread the batter out like a crepe.
4. Cook for 2-3 minutes, flipping when the enchilada tortilla easily separates from the bottom of the pan.
5. Repeat with remaining batter (should make 4-5 enchilada tortillas!)
6. In a medium saucepan, heat 1 Tbsp of oil over medium heat.
7. Add the chicken in slices and cook for 7-10 minutes until fully cooked. Remove chicken and put on a plate to the side.
8. Preheat oven to 350F.
9. In the saucepan, heat another 1 Tbsp of oil on med-high temperature.
10. Dice the onion and add to the pan.
11. Wash and chop the pepper and add to the pan.
12. Finely chop the garlic and add to the pan.
13. Cook on medium temperature until onions are translucent.
14. Add the cumin, chilli powder, chicken and 1/2 cup of enchilada/tomato sauce. Bring to a boil.
15. Simmer for another 2-3 minutes and put aside.
16. Take 1 enchilada tortilla and add 1/4 of the chicken mixture.
17. Roll like a wrap and put into a baking dish. Repeat with remaining 3

tortillas.

18. Add the remaining 2 1/2 cups of enchilada/tomato sauce to the mixture.

19. Bake for 10-12 minutes.

20. Serve & Enjoy!

Breakfast: Paleo Pancakes
SERVES: 2-3
PREP TIME: 5 min
COOK TIME: 20 min

Ingredients:
4 eggs
¼ cup coconut flour
¼ tsp salt
1/2 banana
1 tsp raw cacao powder
2 Tbsp Avocado Oil

Directions:
1. Mash the banana in a medium sized bowl.
2. Add all the other ingredients and mix, not too much until too smooth!
3. Heat 1 Tbsp if oil over medium heat and pour batter when hot for 3-4 minutes on each side.
4. Top with fruit, maple syrup or spread a little almond butter on top!
5. Serve & Enjoy!

Lunch: Paleo style Fajitas
SERVES: 4
PREP TIME: 5 min
COOK TIME: 25 min

Ingredients:
½ LB chicken slices
2 peppers (red or orange)
1 red onion
2 Tbsp Avocado Oil
Sugar-free salsa or homemade paleo salsa
Romaine lettuce

Directions:
1. Heat 2 Tbsp of oil over medium temperature in a saucepan.
2. Add the chicken and cook 7-10 minutes until cooked thoroughly.
3. Remove the chicken and add another 2 Tbsp of oil to the pan.
4. Wash and chop the peppers and add to the pan
5. Dice the onion and add to the pan.
6. Sautee the vegetables for 5-7 minutes and add the chicken slices back into the pan.
7. Add ¼ cup of salsa and cook for another 5 minutes, mixing well.
8. Wash 5 pieces of romaine lettuce and place on a plate.
9. Scoop out chicken fajita mixture into lettuce.
10. Serve & Enjoy!

Dinner: Meat & Potato Bake
SERVES: 2-3
PREP TIME: 5 min
COOK TIME: 1 hr 15 min

Ingredients:
2lb roast beef
2 sweet potatoes
1 medium onion
2 garlic cloves
1 Tbsp cold pressed olive oil
Salt
Pepper

Directions:
1. Preheat oven to 350F.
2. Place the roast beef (best if it's at room temperature) into a large baking dish.
3. Cut the onion into quarters and add to the dish.
4. Wash the sweet potatoes and cut into 1"x1" cubes. Add to the baking dish.
5. Add the garlic cloves whole to the baking dish.
6. Stir the potatoes, onions and cloves around the roast beef with 1 Tbsp olive oil.
7. Sprinkle with salt and pepper.
8. Cook for 60-75 minutes.
9. Serve & Enjoy!

CONGRATULATIONS!

YOU'VE JUST COMPLETED 30 DAYS OF CLEAN EATING WITH THE PALEO DIET!

YOU SHOULD BE VERY PROUD OF YOUR COMMITMENT TO THE CHALLENGE, AND FOR MAKING THE CHOICE TO PUT YOUR HEALTH AND YOUR DIET FIRST IN YOUR LIFE! THAT DESERVES A FEW PATS ON THE BACK!

REMEMBER TO BOOKMARK YOUR FAVOURITE RECIPES FROM THE CHALLENGE FOR QUICK REFERENCING NOW THAT YOU'RE HOOKED AND FEELING GREAT. WHAT A DIFFERENCE IT CAN MAKE TO OUR BODIES WHEN WE EAT REAL FOODS THAT HAVE LITTLE TO NO PROCESSING; THE WAY HUMAN BODIES WERE MEANT TO DIGEST!

A THANK YOU FROM US TO YOU AND MAKE
SURE TO THANK YOURSELF FOR COMPLETING
THE 30 DAY PALEO DIET CHALLENGE!

KEEP PALEO-ING,

TRULY YOURS ELIZABETH VINE

Made in the USA
Lexington, KY
05 April 2016